A Trial by Jury

A Trial by Jury

D. Graham Burnett

Alfred A. Knopf   New York   2001   

This Is a Borzoi Book
Published by Alfred A. Knopf

www.aaknopf.com

Knopf, Borzoi Books, and the colophon are registered
trademarks of Random House, Inc.

Grateful acknowledgment is made to the following for
permission to reprint previously published material:
Alfred A. Knopf: Excerpt from "Anecdote of Men by
the Thousand" from *Collected Poems* by Wallace
Stevens, copyright © 1923 and renewed 1951 by
Wallace Stevens. Reprinted by permission of Alfred
A. Knopf, a division of Random House, Inc.
Ludlow Music, Inc.: Excerpt from "Hangknot, Slipknot,"
words and music by Woody Guthrie, TRO-copyright
© 1963 (renewed) by Ludlow Music, Inc., New York, N.Y.
Reprinted by permission of Ludlow Music, Inc., care
of The Richmond Organization.

ISBN 0-375-41303-0

Manufactured in the United States of America
First Edition

For my parents, my sister,
and a certain lawyer

Tell me who makes the laws for that slipknot?
Who makes the laws for that slipknot?
Who says who is going to the calaboose,
And get the hangman's noose or the slipknot?

Woody Guthrie

Eventually an imaginary world is
entirely without interest.

Wallace Stevens

Note

This book is not a work of fiction. Some dialogue has been reconstructed, and in the interests of privacy and propriety, some names, dates, locations, and personal characteristics have been altered.

Contents

PRELIMINARIES

103 Corlears Street

Randolph Cuffee took the first wound in the chest. And though the chief medical examiner asserted that the incision—vertical, about an inch in length, just to the right of the midline of the sternum—would have required only a "moderate" degree of force, the pathology report drew attention to a noticeable bruise at the top of the cut.

A look at the murder weapon made this easier to understand. The knife (a legal, black-handled folding model with a vicious profile) featured a small metal tab about the size of a shirt button, which stuck out from the side of the blade, opposite the cutting edge, near the handle. Holding the closed knife at the ready placed this stud under the thumb, where it could be used to push the blade into an open and locked position. It was therefore possible to open the knife with one hand.

Possible, not easy. This was not a switchblade; no springs launched the blade. In fact, the maneuver required a certain manual dexterity and strength, since the four fingers had to pin the closed knife against the heel of the hand and draw the handle down into the palm at the same time that the thumb, in opposition, swung the blade (by means of the stud) into readiness; the action could be speeded by a deft snap of the wrist.

These minutiae proved significant. Could Monte Milcray— half naked, lying on his back, his legs "scooped" into the air and flailing (one clamped under each of Cuffee's arms as Cuffee lowered himself into the missionary position over him)—have reached down to the slim tool pocket on the outside right leg of his overalls, liberated the knife clipped there, and then, in the narrow space between their bodies and the futon, executed this one-handed feint and gotten the knife to open?

Put aside the other questions: How could he then have maneuvered the knife (in his right hand) into the space between his torso and that of his alleged attacker, who was at that moment supposedly bearing down on him with all his weight? How, from this awkward position, did Milcray manage such a clean strike? He left not a scratch anywhere else on Cuffee's chest, and yet buried the blade so deeply that the little thumb stud significantly bruised the surrounding tissue. How, in the process, did Milcray manage to make a deep gash on his own *left* shin? And this, curiously, without making any tear in the left leg of his pants?

Put all those questions aside. Ask simply, could he have opened the knife with one hand in that tight corner of the small room with a large man attempting to sodomize him?

The prosecutor ridiculed the idea, taking up the knife (people's exhibit 7) and waving it around the court while badgering the defendant for particulars. In the videotaped testimony, taken shortly after he confessed to the stabbing,

Milcray had used the word "flick" to describe how he opened the knife. For emphasis and dramatic effect, the prosecutor now gave the closed knife a histrionic flick and showed that it remained closed.

From the stand, Milcray—his disarmingly high, effete voice and Southern accent giving him an almost solicitous air—began to gesture helpfully, while trying to explain: "No, not like that, you got to . . ."

"Like this?" asked the prosecutor, making another ineffectual flail.

"No, you got to . . . together . . . flick the wrist and use the stud. . . ."

"Well," cooed the prosecutor, drubbing away at the closed knife with his thumb, and pumping his arm as if he were shaking off a Gila monster, "maybe I'm not so good at it as you. . . ."

Of this there could be little doubt.

Go back eighteen months. On August 2, 1998, around four o'clock in the afternoon, two officers from Manhattan's Sixth Precinct took turns kicking at the door of apartment number one at 103 Corlears Street, a white brick building on the west side of the street between Christopher and West Tenth. When they forced the door (without splitting the jamb or unseating the latch), it opened in and to the right, stopping against a low coffee table and revealing a shallow studio that extended about fifteen feet to each side, but was perhaps only twelve feet deep. Holding back the young man who had brought them to the site, the officers entered the room.

Draped over the dark futon couch before them, and trailing onto the floor to their right, lay two blankets, one a cream-colored knit coverlet, the other a cheap quilted bedspread. Blood spatters stained both. Later, the officers would disagree on the lighting, but they concurred that the television was not on, and that the curtain of the single, street-facing, ground-level window to their right was opaque and closed, with the exception of a small opening in the lower left corner.

Causing this aperture was the lifeless hand of an African-American male, about six feet tall and slightly under two hundred pounds. The body lay facedown, the head wedged between the arm of the futon and the radiator under the window, the legs splayed into the middle of the room. Rigor mortis had cemented a tableau of the victim's final gesture: the right arm reaching up to the sill, surely an effort to pull himself to the window and call for help. Under the left arm lay a wig of long, dark, kinky hair. The body was naked.

The officers testified that they did not approach the figure or check for vital signs. Twenty-odd stab wounds along the right side of the victim's spine, neck, and head persuaded them from across the room of what the assistant medical examiner would confirm several hours later: Randolph Cuffee, "Antigua," a habitué of the Watutsi Lounge, and a familiar face in the other gay bars of the West Village, was dead.

Not, however, until later, when crime-scene investigators pulled the stiffened body into the middle of the room and rolled it over, did anyone see the wound that actually killed him—that thin and nearly bloodless slit at his sternum, which, reaching two and a half inches into the thoracic cavity, had just "nicked" (in the word of the chief medical examiner) the upper arch of the aorta. Within minutes of the blow, misplaced blood would have filled the sac around the heart, choking off its beat, a condition known as an "acute traumatic cardiac tamponade." It is as if the heart drowns. Immobility follows, and death shortly thereafter.

Also revealed when the body was moved: two braided leather whips and two unrolled condoms, one inside the other.

PART I

The Open Court

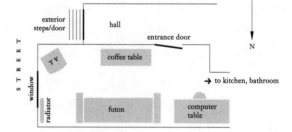

1. How It Ended

I have on my desk at this moment twelve five-by-seven ruled index cards. On each of them the same two words appear: "not guilty." Eight are written in pen, four in pencil. On eight of them the words appear along a single line, on two the words are perpendicular to the ruling, and on two they are scrawled diagonally (one of these last has been written on an inverted card, turned so that the red top line and margin are at the bottom). Three are in all caps, three have only the initial letters capitalized, three are all lowercase, two others show the "N" capitalized but not the "g." In the last of them the word "NOT" appears in all caps, but the word "guilty" is all lowercase.

By dint of these varied inscriptions, made in silence in a few tense moments, Monte Virginia Milcray walked out of Part 24 of the New York State Supreme Court, got into the elevator, and descended to the cold wetness of Centre Street a little before noon on February 19, 2000. I preceded him by several minutes, getting into a cab with my duffel bag and riding the dozen blocks home to my wife, with whom I had not spoken in four days. The cards were folded in the breast pocket of my navy blazer. I was crying.

The twelve cards represent the potent residue of the most intense sixty-six hours of my life, a period during which I served as the foreman of a jury charged to decide whether Monte Milcray was guilty of murdering Randolph Cuffee. During that period, twelve individuals of considerable diversity engaged in a total of twenty-three hours of sustained conversation in a small, bare room. We ran the gamut of group dynamics: a clutch of strangers yelled, cursed, rolled on the floor, vomited, whispered, embraced, sobbed, and invoked both God and necromancy. There were moments when the scene could have passed for a graduate seminar in political theory, others that might have been a jujitsu class. A few came straight out of bedlam. Before it was over, we had spent three nights and four days continuously attended by armed guards (who extended their affable surveillance into all lavatories); we had been shuttled to outlying hotels, into rooms with disconnected phones and sinks in which we washed our clothes; we had watched one juror pulled from our midst and rushed to the hospital (a physical collapse, caused by some combination of missing medication and the crucible of the deliberations), another make a somewhat half-hearted effort to escape (he was apprehended), and a third insist on her right to contact her own lawyer to extricate her from the whole affair (she was threatened with contempt).

During significant stretches in this trying time, we considered two weeks of testimony in *The People of New York* v. *Monte Virginia Milcray* and struggled to understand two things: what happened in Cuffee's apartment on the night of

August 1, 1998, and what responsibilities we had as citizens and jurors.

It is my intention to tell this story as best I can. I am doing so for several reasons, among them two in particular: first, because there are things to be learned from the way events unfolded (about people, about the law, about justice, about truth and how we know it), and, second, because the jury room is a most remarkable—and largely inaccessible—space in our society, a space where ideas, memories, virtues, and prejudices clash with the messy stuff of the big, bad world. We expect much of this room, and we think about it less often than we probably should.

Before I embark on this task, however, a few words of warning. There are really two stories here: that of the case itself—a trial story, a courtroom story, a drama focused on a violent death; and that of the deliberations—the story of what happened behind the closed door of the jury room. Each of these stories is complex, and they are of course entangled. I set out to write this book in order to tell the latter, but to do so I must rehearse elements of the former. Let me be clear, though: it is by no means my intention to retry the case in a personal memoir. The case is closed. In writing this book, I have made no additional investigations of the events at issue, I have not revisited the records of the trial, and I have not interviewed any of the people involved. All of that was tempting, and would certainly have been interesting, but my sense has been that to embark on such digging would have been, inevitably, to put the trial on trial, to lose myself again in the twisting labyrinth of unrecoverable fact that we negotiated in the jury room. I would have begun to extend that labyrinth, to open new rooms and passages. And this was not the aim. I am sure there is more to the maze than I have seen (when is there not?), but by keeping notes during the weeks of the trial, I laid a thread along the path we took together as jurors, and that is the thread I will follow here.

A further disclaimer: what I am writing is my own story of the deliberations. I have no idea what those who shared the experience with me would make of this document should they pick it up. Or let me speak more frankly: I am sure each of them would contest my story in different ways—argue, perhaps, that I did not represent them rightly; assert that this part over here was not that way; draw to my attention things I have forgotten. If one learns anything from a criminal trial under the adversary system, it is that sincere folk can differ vehemently about events, and that there is seldom any easy way to figure out what actually went on.

At different moments while writing this account—much of it longhand in a notebook during the weeks following the acquittal—I have closed my eyes and tried to imagine what the small, bare jury room looked like from the perspective of the others. We sat around the same table, but the room must have appeared slightly different to each. I try to see in my mind's eye how things looked from the other side—the door on one's right, the winter windows at one's back.

That is where Dean Kossler sat. What would he think of this narrative? Dean—the big, solid, former bull-riding cowboy turned vacuum-cleaner repairman. Dean—the six-foot-three-inch born-again God-fearing veteran of the U.S. armed forces. When I first noticed him, in the early days of jury selection, he was spitting tobacco juice behind the radiator by the elevator during a break. He had thin brown hair slicked back and a manly mustache; he wore a weathered pair of work boots. A blowhard contractor of some sort, I assumed, and I pegged him, without much thought, as a poster boy for Susan Faludi's tragic tale of the white working-class male—big chest, big gut, big debt. I called him, irreverently, "the Faludiman" in my notes. What did I know? Before the trial ended, he had blown my stereotype (indeed, any stereotype) wide open.

What would he say about all this? About what I have written?

Or Felipe Rodriguez? I originally wrote to myself that he seemed "sweet and shy." He giggled often, wore a large number of braided string bracelets, seemed lost in his giant orange parka. I came to loathe him. By the end, he had thrown much into question for me: not least, my confidence in jury trials. Are there some citizens not clearly able to distinguish daytime television from daily life? Apparently there are. Should they participate in deciding on the freedom of another person? Maybe. I doubt he remembers things as I do.

And there were others, of course. Leah Tennent, the self-possessed and buoyantly bohemian young woman with whom I read Wallace Stevens poems in the back of the bus. Olivelle "Vel" Tover, the youthful, clear-eyed black woman with an elaborate braided coiffure who studied a manual of purgative and rejuvenating fasts in the waiting area; we discussed together the value of self-denial, of cleansing the body through the strictest diets. Rachel Patis, the solid, quiet, unflappable West Indian woman who volunteered at her local police precinct and wore blouses trimmed with lace; she moved slowly, sat very still, seemed like an older lady. Patricia Malley, "Pat," the dyed-blonde tough-girl in the tight black jeans who spoke loudly and much, often well;

she seemed instantly animated in Dean's company, adjusted her eyeliner, laughed easily and with gusto.

And so on: James Lanes (who went by Jim), Jessica Pollero, Suzy O'Mear, Paige Barri, and Adelle Benneth. This last was, like me, a professor of history. More improbable still, she focused, as I do, on the history of science, and had, like me, a particular interest in exploration and travel narratives (though she worked on the medieval period and I on the modern). A striking coincidence, all this.

Together, then, we were two professional historians (Adelle and I), two ad-copy writers (Jessica and Jim), a globe-trotting Gen-X software developer (Leah), an industrial-vacuum-cleaner repairman with a rodeo tattoo who moonlighted in car-stereo installation (Dean), an interior decorator (Paige), an "independent marketing executive" and part-time security guard (Rachel), an actress (Pat, but was she also a bartender?), the manager of certain commercial enterprises owned by the "Mattress King of Miami" (Vel), and a couple of others (Felipe, Suzy) of less clear occupation. Twelve citizens, twelve different characters.

The deliberations were theirs as much as mine. This story, however, is mine alone. Like a witness, I am fallible; I shall surely misremember things. And even if my memory were perfect, what retelling, in a string of words, is not a distressing distortion of the cluttered thickness of things as they happen?

Trials are about this.

2. How It Began

At the start, I decided to treat the unwelcome interruption of jury duty as something like a vacation, a brief visit to a foreign country of bureaucratic languor and vast waiting rooms, a linoleum land inhabited by a genuine demographic cross section of the Big Apple. Plus, I could get some reading done. There was a certain irony to this. My job, in fact, was a one-year fellowship in a well-appointed humanities center at a large New York institution of learning—books everywhere, a silent and bright office without a phone, distinguished colleagues, catered lunches. My only formal responsibilities were to read and write. But things piled up on the desk—student evaluations, article proofs needing attention, endless e-mail—so the New York State Criminal Court began to look like an opportunity to hide in plain view.

Actually ending up on a jury never crossed my mind. The day before I reported for duty I had a conversation with a friend in Chicago, a logician, who claimed that the magic word was "philosophy": once the lawyers heard it, you were kindly asked to leave. I figured introducing myself as an intellectual historian ought to have the same effect. With a legal-scholar wife who had worked for the public defender's office (and contributed to a lawyers' manual on death-penalty defense), I promised to give any healthy prosecutor hives. I brought along a copy of *The New York Review of Books* just in case.

My juror card instructed me to appear at 9 a.m., but it is later than that when I finally clear the metal detectors and the low-ceilinged lobby of the dingy Centre Street court building and find my way upstairs.

All the public spaces seem crowded with people, still bundled against the cold, slush melting into muddy pools at their feet as they stand around, waiting. I catch a fragment of a conversation between two older Hispanic women in the elevator: "Just two ounces! Not some *kilo* or noth'n . . . But he didn't care. . . ."

In the twice-exhaled air of the jury waiting room, about two hundred disgruntled New Yorkers had arranged themselves like a tray of magnetic monopoles: maximum space between each particle and its neighbors. Some read newspapers, others books; a few students had staked out desks in the corner and had begun to study, wearing Walkmans. Most simply stared into space. As seems to happen oddly often in New York crowds, I recognized someone (or thought I did): a guy I had played pickup basketball with several times at an uptown gym on the West Side. The city, finally, is finite; it takes several years to notice this.

Centre Street's hostile levee of potential jurors is daily called to attention by the senior court clerk, Victor Spellsman, a tousle-headed, squint-eyed Brooklyn native gone prematurely gray. He seems to be well on his way to becoming a

New York institution, as attested by the gallery of inscribed celebrity headshots on the wall outside his office. (Gwyneth Paltrow! Stephen Jay Gould?) And rightly so. Combining precise measures of camp-counselor patience and "fuhgedaboudit" irascibility, he got the headphones off everyone, got the newspapers put away, and took people through the drill, demonstrating the use of the octagonal lottery-roller that would determine who got called up for which panel.

Victor had questions for us: "Any convicted felons in the room?" he boomed happily. Sniggers. "No need to jump up," he added hastily, with the honed timing of a natural stand-up, "just wander into the clerk's office down the hall a little later, and I'll let you go."

"Anybody not understand English?" he mumbled indistinctly, waving his arm over us. He asked this so fast I hardly caught it. But quite a few people promptly rose, and began making their way to the front to get their release cards. Out they filed.

The joke grew on people. Bemused murmuring.

Victor shook his head.

"I'll never understand it," he stage-whispered to the rest of us, as a heavyset woman bulled for the double doors.

After details (location of restrooms, water fountain, snack machine; an exhortation not to steal the magazines), we settled in to watch the preparatory video, narrated by Ed Bradley and Diane Sawyer. In addition to offering canned testimonials to the effect that we were going to have a great time (and a civics lesson, too), the program set jury duty in its historical context. This was compressed in the extreme, and got under way with a memorable flashback to the dark days of the trial by ordeal: As Sawyer's woodwind voice soothingly narrated the bleak realities of justice in a benighted age, a knot of stringy-haired plebes, smirched and scrofulous, dragged a bound man through the woods and cast him into a deep lake. A papist factotum solemnly made the sign of the cross over the disappearance of the accused, and we learned that he would be found innocent if he did not resurface. Not an outtake from *Monty Python*, but an educational film prepared by the state of New York, the dramatization ended with the suggestion that the accused was innocent, and that his kinsmen may have succeeded in recovering him from the bottom.

The movie put everyone in a good mood, and strongly suggested the possibility of human progress in matters juridical. The Centre Street court building was grim and forbidding in a Stalinist sort of way (towering, gray, squint-windowed), but it clearly beat the heck out of the Inquisition. I went back to my review.

As the morning wore on, certain tremors manifested themselves in the taciturn atmosphere of the waiting room: while many read, worked, paid bills, zoned out into the world of their headphones, talked on cellular phones (Victor: "We do the cell phones in the *hall*, right? Show a little *con-sid-er-AY-tion!*"), or perused the increasingly grubby newspapers that made the rounds, still others seemed to eye the field. Though initially annoying, yes, this whole business was legal hooky, after all. One sensed a few people beginning to warm to the prospects, to the idea that they were not in their offices—indeed, that their not being at work was a *civic duty*, and one positively remunerated (albeit at a rather sorry level). Moreover, the room was full of other people, some of them attractive, all of them in similar circumstances—namely, trapped in close proximity, and for the most part deeply bored. Conveniently, a natural topic of conversation—the pains of jury duty—presented itself. There was a somewhat funny movie on the subject to discuss, and plenty of openings for sympathetic chitchat on the inconvenience of it all, and neighborly mutterings on the bureaucratic sclerosis of city and state government. A few strategic relocations could be witnessed; casual glances followed, saw reciprocation. By late morning, several conversational couples had formed, and these developed naturally into informal luncheon dates when we were directed to the neighborhood restaurants of our choosing and told to return in an hour and a half.

I walked home for lunch, thinking I had learned something already: the Manhattan jury-duty waiting room secreted an unexpected libidinous energy. At this rate, if the wait lengthened to a threatened third day, I could visualize lubricious scenes in the green halls.

And it was January yet. In spring, I decided, the wheels of justice must grind to a halt.

I missed the chance to follow these developments. In the afternoon my name came up in a group of about seventy people mustered for the selection process in Part 24.

It was shortly after entering that I first saw Milcray, when the judge asked him to turn around in his chair and face the courtroom. He did so. We saw a slim, dark-skinned black man who seemed exceedingly young. (He was twenty-one.) His hair trimmed close, he wore a black-and-white shirt, striped horizontally—a shirt of his own, but one that strongly suggested prison attire. He had a tendency to let his right hand linger at his chin, partially obscuring his face.

Did any of us recognize this man? No one moved. Milcray turned back around. Satisfied, the judge began to read a list of names: witnesses and investigators in the case, locations and establishments. Already the attorneys, seated at their unmatched tables below the bench, were craning their heads behind them, casting their eyes over us, counting and assessing.

Space is plastic in the mind. A room can change shape. Part 24 of the New York Supreme Court warped perceptibly for me when the judge announced that *The People of New York* v. *Monte Virginia Milcray* would be a trial for murder. We sat in a double-height hall with a bright northern exposure and blonded oak wainscoting reaching halfway up the white walls. Only behind the judge's seat did this paneling extend to the beamed ceiling, creating a lofty frame where brushed metal letters announced "In God We Trust." The invocation confirmed the sacral architecture: the altarlike bench, the choirlike jury box, the lecternlike witness stand, the rood screen of the balustrade separating the congregation in their pews from the powerful seats beyond.

When the judge announced that we were trying Milcray for murder, this link, between his name and that word, introduced a new point of gravity in the room, distorting the pious front-facing quality of the space. It was as if the floor under the defense's table had suddenly sunk into a strange deflection at the impact of a heavy, hidden object. We were now in a room with two gravitational centers: the judge and the defendant. This curious feeling was strongest at that moment, but it never entirely vanished. An accused person, standing in a court of law, has, somehow, tremendous weight.

Years past, in an archaically formal Catholic grammar school, I participated in competitive poetic declamation. To the chagrin of several rotund nuns, I settled firmly on Oscar

Wilde's "The Ballad of Reading Gaol" as the text I would perform at our interacademy meet. A tale of lust and slaughter ("for each man kills the thing he loves") set against the tragic story of Wilde's own imprisonment (for unnatural acts of manly affection), it was not, properly speaking, suitable stuff for the sixth grade. Nor did the judges at Devon Preparatory School on Philadelphia's staid Main Line warm to my impassioned recitation ("And blood and wine were on his hands / When they found him with the dead"). My delivery received respectable marks, but notes on my score sheets suggested I seek out new material.

And yet the lines stuck deep in my head. The shock of hearing the word "murder" while looking at Milcray triggered a flash of poetic memory: Wilde's swooning exclamation on learning that the man he spies in the prison yard faces punishment for a capital offense. The lines read:

> *Dear Christ! The very prison walls*
> *Suddenly seemed to reel,*
> *And the sky above my head became*
> *Like a casque of scorching steel. . . .*

Romantic excess, surely. But I was learning at that moment in Part 24 what Wilde-the-convict knew well in Reading: the environments of state power—courts, prisons—heighten ordinary emotions. For the next month, each day would underline the lesson. One is vulnerable here, made small; an aura of finality pricks out the details of ordinary life; a large force waits in the wings.

The room grew quiet for a moment. But only for a moment, for, as soon as the judge moved on to explain that the trial would take more than a week, and that it would involve sequestration, up went a distinct and concerned murmur. When the judge invited those who believed themselves incapable of fulfilling such an obligation to come forward and explain, 80 percent of the room rose. I whispered to the woman sitting next to me that I was a little surprised more people weren't curious to see what would happen; she said she was only remaining seated while she thought up an excuse. My sense was that I was busy, but how could I be too busy for this? Unlike many of those trying to be excused, I faced no particular financial hardship if I ended up being asked to serve. One by one people approached the bench, mumbled, and were dismissed. This took the remainder of the day.

I slipped out to the men's room down the hall. On the filthy wall two choice bits of graffiti stood out: "Fuck the police" and "I sniff juror underpants."

The following morning, after my name found its way out of yet another octagonal roller, I was called from the pews and seated in the jury box. The process of selection now began in earnest: this was *voir dire*, the question-and-answer session that the attorneys use to select jurors; I was on the "panel." We were a total of eighteen, but our number required repeated replenishing as panelists disqualified themselves and the judge asked them to step down. Some cases were stranger than others. A shuffling man in a flannel shirt carrying a plastic bag of books and dog-eared papers declared lucidly that he was a Quaker, and that his religion prevented him from being part of "any process that authorizes the government to use violence against any individual." He was excused.

Several of our number bowed out in response to the simple question, "Is there anyone here who believes that they are unable to be fair in judging this case?" The clean-cut young man next to me, with a spy thriller on his lap, raised his hand. "And why not?" Because he felt that recidivism rates were too high, and he "basically" didn't want it on his conscience if the guy killed again. Anyway, he thought the best policy was to lock 'em all up for good.

Killed again? We hadn't even figured out if he'd killed the first time. Excused.

One woman said she was terrified, afraid of being involved; she was hyperventilating. Excused.

A hand went up. A soccer-mom type, well put together, energetic. On being asked to explain, she tripped over her tongue and could say only that she did not think she could be fair, "in the circumstances."

"What circumstances?" the judge wanted to know.

"Just . . . well, being here," she stuttered, gesturing at the room. She could not find the words.

The judge dismissed her with undisguised irritation. But as she gathered her bag and coat, I found myself wondering if she hadn't grasped something real and disturbing about the proceedings. After all, the judge had said we needed to be "impartial," that we were not to let the fact that the defendant had been arrested have any weight as we evaluated his guilt or innocence. But what could this rhetoric of neutrality possibly mean, here, in the *"circumstances,"* literally, "that which stood around us"—the vaulting room, the somber judge, the armed guards? We sat in a theater trimmed with the trappings of the state's power; this power was being dramatized for us with pomp. Yet the judge wanted us to deny that any of this—his high chair, the robes, the guns—would influence our perception. But how could it not? The state (that is, the prosecution) had decided that Monte Milcray was guilty, and this was the state's stage. The woman scurried out, too careful, I decided, to play along with our collective fib.

Next we ran through a cycle of biographical questions, which each of us was expected to answer rapidly, in turn: occupation; length of time lived in Manhattan; previous jury experience; friends, family, or close acquaintances in law enforcement or the legal profession; had we ever been the victim of a crime?

When the occupation question came to me, I said I was a "professor of intellectual history."

The judge looked up. "Where do you teach?" he asked.

Hesitating, I said I was not currently teaching, but had been, until this year, at Columbia.

He made a mark on the sheet in front of him. I felt nervous, afraid of my voice in the room. What we were doing seemed impossibly grave.

I glanced at Milcray, whose half-smiling face and lively eyes followed every exchange closely.

Very few of the people on the panel had no previous experience of crime. In bare phrases people shared fragments of large stories: family friend killed; got mugged twice, apartment robbed; held at gunpoint, robbed; car stolen, house robbed.

I said, "Two cars stolen, house robbed."

In my wallet I still carried the insurance card from a brick-red '67 Chrysler Newport that had disappeared from a parking place on Osage Avenue in front of my house in West Philadelphia on a Thanksgiving morning many years earlier. I came out into the holiday air with a canister of auto-body cement and an orbital sander to do some work on a ding in the passenger-side door, and stood there stupidly, looking at the spot where I had left the car. Had my convertible dream turned into a blue pickup? For some inexplicable reason, I got down on my knees and looked under the truck.

The judge explained the standard of proof. The state must prove its case beyond a reasonable doubt. Did we hear that? This did not mean mathematical certainty, but simply beyond the doubt of a reasonable person. "Is there anyone here," the judge continued, "who would hold the state to an *unreasonable* standard?"

In my heightened state I felt a strange, somewhat manic delight. Most of my academic life had been spent studying the history of what people found reasonable—from alchemical conjurations to statistical facts. The history of science is, in a way, the history of what proofs have counted as "reasonable" in different communities at different moments. To agree on what is true—about nature, about God—has again and again proved a tall order, and the standard of "the reasonable man" was, I knew, yet another invention (like the laboratory, the footnote, the College of Cardinals) to make the difficult task of truth-seeking a little easier in certain contexts—courts of law in particular. It was a much-contested question, this business of who-all was "reasonable," and what, precisely, such a person looked like. There was a history here.

But there I was. No time to pontificate, to remonstrate, to have a seminar. My ponderous classroom musings on Pascal or the Enlightenment were not welcome. I had to act as if I knew what "reasonable" meant, or raise my hand. For a moment the very thing seemed to be made real and hover before me. The ideal of the mind. Reason. Now we would all be reasonable. No more epistemological fretting or historicist relativism—the greatest abstraction in human affairs had just taken shape and entered the room. I kept my hand in my lap. If all the others thought they were going to be reasonable, then, hell, I thought, I can be just as reasonable as anybody else.

No one moved. Reason had been installed, deftly, quickly, in a second of silence. We moved on.

The judge introduced the next question with a short explanation of how responsibilities would be divided in the trying of the case: "It is the function of the jury to apply the *law* to the *evidence* in the case. You will be the judge of the facts, but I am the judge of the law. It is not the function of a jury to rule on the law itself. You are to apply the law whether you agree with it or not, whether you think it is a good law or a bad one. Do any of you have a problem with this?"

There was a pause.

I raised my hand.

"Mr. . . . Burnett," he said, reading from his chart. "What is your problem with this?"

And I replied, my throat tight, that if I thought the defendant would face the death penalty I might be inclined to acquit, even if I thought him guilty.

My anxiety about speaking had only increased: the judge had just humiliated one of the panelists, a young well-to-do woman with long brown hair and a tendency to mumble. On an earlier question he gave her two chances to speak up and then scolded her harshly for wasting the court's time. Sitting there with a little Prada handbag in her lap, she looked completely shocked. Her expression suggested no one had ever been rude to her before. But the judge did not relent—he laid into her again, as she stuttered.

My throat tightened, too, from the certainty that my statement would disqualify me from service. This made me sad: once I had glimpsed the way the trial would force the prettiest abstractions into actual and fateful practice, I was completely absorbed—aware that this was a rare opportunity to participate in something important, weighty, real, something very different from my academic life. At the same time, I had resolved to be entirely straight with every question, and I could not promise in advance that I would apply a law that took human life.

The judge expressed no interest. The death penalty was not relevant in this case, he announced dismissively, and opened the floor to the lawyers.

The lead prosecutor—heavy, bald, with a distinctive spot of livid skin under his left eye—approached first, greeted us, and began to ask questions, some general, posed to the group, some addressed specifically to one panelist or another, in response to information we had given about our jobs, or previous experiences of crime or jury duty. He wanted to make sure we would give his witnesses a fair hearing, regardless of what they were wearing or how they talked. Did any of us think that homosexual people had a particular tendency to lie? No one moved. He directed the question specifically to the older man now sitting to my right, the only one of us in a suit, a gold Rolex on his left wrist, his hands neatly folded in his lap. He shook his head and said no, adding, slightly defensively, that he was an openly gay man, who lived an openly gay life and had for years. He wore a cabochon garnet pinky ring. He would be, initially, our foreman, until he vanished in the last days of the trial.

Harder to interpret than these questions was the next: "Do any of you think it is possible for a man to have sex with another man and not be gay?"

Several of us must have looked puzzled, because he tried

to clarify: "Do any of you think it is possible for a man to have sex with another man and not think of himself as a gay man?"

This made sense. The answer seemed obvious to me: sure. No one responded. I raised my hand.

"You think that *is* possible?" he repeated, and I said I did. What made me say that? he wondered. I replied that there was plenty of evidence that different cultures at different points in history thought different ways about same-sex unions. For instance, in South America there were traditions in which it was considered exceedingly masculine to have sex with some men in some ways. (The phrase had always stuck in my head: "*Soy tan macho que me cojo otros hombres.*")

"OK . . ." the prosecutor said slowly. "OK," he repeated, looking around the panel.

Did anyone else have knowledge of this sort of research, or agree that this was possible? Two or three hands went up. Who knows what he was getting at with this line of questioning. I never understood what relevance it had to the case.

Less pale than his adversary, the defense attorney had a slightly nasal (if not actually whiny) voice, and a tendency to lean back in his chair, legal pad on his knee, and gaze over our heads, out the window high up behind the jury box. He rose, came still closer, rested his elbows on the bar in front of the jury box. In an intimate way, sighing as if commiserating with our plight, he said slowly, "Good morning."

There was little reply.

From his questions the contours of the case itself began to emerge for the first time. Did any of us think that it was impossible for a man to rape another man? Silence. Did any of us think that a man who legitimately thought he was going to be raped should not, could not, use any means at his command to protect himself? He looked at us closely. No one raised a hand.

"Now," he said suddenly, breaking his eye contact and moving away from the rail, "there were a lot of stab wounds"— sounding the last two words as if he were shrugging with his voice—"twenty-five, twenty-six stab wounds . . . and a lot of these were in the back. Are there any of you who think, right now, that it's just *impossible*, that if you were defending yourself, and you were in a dark room, and there is this man, on top of you, trying to sodomize you—are there any of you who just say, 'No way! There's *no way* you could stab somebody *twenty-five times* in self-defense'?" He looked back at us, and let the question sink in.

This was the first we heard of the wounds.

After several seconds, a large woman in the second row, heavily made up, raised her hand. "You, you think that's just *impossible?*" he continued. "I mean, you're excited, you're scared. . . ."

She furrowed her prominent brow and thought about it, and as she did so it was clear that she was slow. But she stuck to her guns. You couldn't put this one over on her— something was fishy about that number.

Fair enough, I thought. But I could swallow the idea. I had seen fights where people were trying to do each other serious harm. I had even been in one or two such fights. It was hard to put a limit on what might happen under those circumstances.

They sent us into the hall to wait. A few people chatted. I kept to myself. When we were called back into the room, it all happened very fast. The judge read five names, including mine and that of the man next to me, the white-haired gentleman with the garnet and the Rolex, Richard Chorst. I looked at him and shrugged, assuming we had been dismissed. But then the other thirteen panelists were asked to rise and follow the bailiff. And suddenly the five of us were standing, and the clerk of count was reading us the oath, and we were sworn jurors.

I cannot remember the oath, but the clerk I see clearly: knobby, long, and mournful, his eyes furtive under bushy white brows, a desultory necktie hanging loosely at the collar of his worn-thin dress shirt—Thomas Mackelwee, associate clerk of count. He would sit at his desk in the corner of the courtroom as the trial wore on, dozing sometimes, quietly reading the *Post*, which he laid unobtrusively flat over his papers, getting up to swear in witnesses in his deferential mumble. Once, he was called on by the judge to give the dimensions of the courtroom in yards, to help a witness specify a key distance estimate in his testimony. Thomas Mackelwee was deep asleep. Uncharacteristically, the judge did not lose his temper. He paused, looked up, and called for a recess. Some people chuckled, but he did not.

Thomas and the judge were two old, old men; one sensed they had worked together for a long time.

One afternoon Thomas approached me in the hall and said, his eyes skittish, that he was interested in history.

I liked him a good deal.

It would be another four days before we heard a word of evidence: it would take four more panels to round out a full complement of jurors and alternates. The judge does nothing to make this delay any easier on those of us picked first. Friday, Monday, Tuesday, Wednesday, we show up, and wait.

And wait, still in the hall, as a trickle is added to our number after each long round of selection. For a while there is, among us, a woman reading a book of Camus short stories. Then she stops showing up.

One afternoon (we are seven now who have been sworn in) I walk to the Canal Street subway stop with a fellow juror, picked the second day, Jessica Pollero, who wears elegant knit dresses with bold geometric patterns and carries a large pigskin bag. Is she in her early thirties? A streak of gray in her dark, full hair may be deceptive; but so, too (in the other direction), her flawless complexion. She writes advertising copy for a city agency, but wants to go freelance. We talk about France (she found the people rude), and the location of a restaurant in the Village (is it too close to the scene of the killing for her to go? The judge keeps warning us to stay away from the area, but she has plans). She is very nice, but less exotic, somehow, than I had imagined. Later, she would grow interested in a television show that involved marrying a millionaire. She sought the opinion of other jurors on this show: Could we believe it?

I do not own a television, and this was to surprise her.

Each day ends the same way: tomorrow we ought to get going. One of us, the quiet guy named Jim Lanes, freaks out on Tuesday and starts yelling at the bailiff after roll call, saying he isn't waiting around anymore, and isn't coming back. At first the officer tries to soothe him, and then, when that has no effect, gets serious, telling him that he is subject to arrest if he leaves.

Lanes is a nice man in his mid-forties, handsome, and dressed in a tastefully quirky way—a chocolate-brown houndstooth shirt and an elegant maroon bow tie with white fletches. We chat going down in the infuriatingly slow elevator. His advertising business is a partnership with his wife, a designer. For all his dashing appearance he is quiet, polite, almost retiring in conversation. In this light his anger earlier seems bizarre, sudden, exaggerated.

Paige Barri wears clogs, and red socks that sparkle; she talks on the phone in the hall a great deal, and seems to be friendly already with Leah Tennent, who is taller, the same twenty-something age, carries a backpack, has a kaffiyeh scarf whorled rakishly at her neck. They go out for coffee, and are always the last to come skidding down the hall when we are asked to assemble in the court. I overhear Paige trying to explain to the bailiff that she has some kind of class on Thursday afternoons.

She *can* miss it, but . . .

Paige is the interior decorator; her temperament is cool, a touch disinterested, slightly impatient. Leah's software company designs multi-player games, but she talks about the job like it's a lark, something she is just trying out for fun. She has traveled a good deal (South America, East Asia) and had some adventures. There is a bounce in her step, and her lively green eyes narrow slyly when she smiles, which she does often, brightly, with a hint of mischief.

For my part, I dress way down, since the court building is so dusty and rank—parachute pants, hiking boots, a fleece. The rough index for my first book has come back from the press, so I fill the time in the hallway by poring over the loose galley pages, making index annotations. I am blandly friendly, but sit alone.

It is late Wednesday afternoon when we get under way, filing into the open court down the main aisle, preceded by the bailiff, who announces our entry by barking, "The jury is in the court!" as the metal door swings open; faces turn to observe. For the first time we see the victim's family, arranged in the penultimate row of the courtroom, on the prosecutor's side. When we are assembled, Richard Chorst, the neat gentleman with the garnet ring, gets placed in the first seat, with me on his left. He sits upright, his hands folded in his lap. He, the judge explains, will be our foreman.

"Are these jurors satisfactory to the people?" the judge asks the prosecutor, and he replies, without looking at us, "Satisfactory to the people." "And to the defense?" The answer comes, a pinched voice, as the lawyer shuffles files: "Yes, your honor."

And we begin.

3. The Defendant

From the first moments of the prosecution's opening statement, the strange nature of the proceedings made a deep impression. How did it happen, I wondered, that a practice of truth-seeking had evolved to divide the job up in all these curious ways? The asking of questions was reserved to those who would play no role in judging the answers, while we, the jury, who were supposed to try to figure out what had gone on, had to remain absolutely silent. And though it was up to us to decide if the defendant was guilty, we would have no part in determining the consequences of that decision: the business of setting punishments was reserved to the judge; we wouldn't even know what they might be. (Although, later, during a suspension in our deliberations, when we were held temporarily in an empty courtroom under loose guard, one of us milling around the vacant bench found a judge's laminated sheet of "sentencing guidelines"; thus we learned what would happen to Milcray if we convicted—he could go to prison for life.)

Our enforced silence was the most difficult thing. How could one even begin to investigate a problem without being able to engage with it directly? We were allowed no paper or writing implements. I fidgeted like a monkey.

The prosecution's first witness was Antigua's sister—catatonic, blank, her thick West Indian accent clipping her monosyllabic answers.

"And did you go to the morgue with the police?"

"Yes."

"And did they show you the body at that time?"

"Yes."

"And did you recognize the body?"

"Yes."

"And was it the body of Randolph Cuffee, 'Antigua,' your brother?"

"It was me broth'r," she said, beginning to sob in stoic stillness.

"And what did you say?"

The judge cut off this question: "It is not relevant what she said," he announced irritably. "Next question . . ."

My way up Centre Street in the evening takes me past the adjacent jail, linked by a bridge of sighs to the court building itself. I step aside to let one of the repainted school buses of the Corrections Department back into the loading dock. It pings insistently and has windows of metal mesh. Milcray may ride in one of these. He may be held in the jail at night. We are not told.

Paused, I notice an interesting architectural detail on the building: the squared-off columns posed decoratively around its base are constructed of wire, as if they were the armature of a plaster sculpture. Harmless enough, modernist, and not unattractive. But, looking more closely, I see this means that these columns, set before the jailhouse, appear to be composed of stacks of little barred cells. I sense a tendentious architect slipping a caustic commentary past his clients: the traditional elegant white columns of the classical orders (those symbols of justice, and props to the pediment of the republic), stripped bare, reveal a carceral skeleton. Unnerving.

After police discovered the body of Randolph Cuffee, they followed standard procedures in the investigation of a stabbing death: they canvassed New York–area hospitals for patients admitted with cuts to their arms and hands. It is hard to stab someone many times, in haste and agitation, and avoid a slip or two.

Monte Milcray slipped. He had been admitted to St. Vincent's Hospital around 2 a.m. on August 2 after being picked up by police near Sheridan Square. Central Dispatch had sent a squad car to follow up on the report of a young African-American man with an ugly hand wound who was making his way along the outdoor cafés of the neighborhood asking anyone with a cell phone to call 911. His right pinky was more or less severed, and there was a good deal of blood on his overalls, his shoes, and his personal effects.

When investigators pulled the file on this incident, they saw a suspicious story. Milcray had told the responding officers (who called in the paramedics) that he had been in an extended altercation with "five white males," a posse that initially confronted him outside his gym in the Flatiron District, and then pursued him on a wild chase, punctuated by beatings, all the way down to an area he vaguely indicated lay to the west on Christopher Street. Shaking them finally (though having managed to conserve his hip pack, its water bottles, a CD Walkman, and his jacket), Milcray discovered his hand injury and sought help. Where was his shirt? Lost in the fight. Had he tried to alert passers-by or duck into an attended building during the twenty-five-block bias crime? Apparently not. Could he describe the attackers? Loosely at best.

It is hard to come up with a good lie. Monte Milcray immediately became the leading suspect in the death of Randolph Cuffee. This was not, of course, how police then approached him. Rather, the detectives who visited him in his hospital room expressed a desire to learn more about his own assailants, and asked permission to take his bag and shoes to the lab in order to run some tests that might aid in this investigation. Meanwhile, the precinct sent two intrepid gumshoes to a medical-waste incinerator on Long Island, where they spent several hours picking over the contents of a large dump truck in an effort to recover Milcray's overalls, which the hospital had discarded. Amazingly, they succeeded. Later, most of these items would prove to be splattered with a mixture of human bloods: Milcray's and Cuffee's.

When Milcray came out of surgery the next day, his finger largely reconnected, he was asked if he would be willing to take a ride down to the station house in order to look over some photos, in hopes of making an identification. He agreed, and was shuttled to a neighboring precinct, because cameras and press reporters were on stakeout at the Sixth, clamoring for a break in the Cuffee case. The specter of a gay-bashing incident had attracted much attention.

The two lead detectives in the case put Milcray in a small, windowless interrogation room with a spy-through mirror and gave him a can of lemonade and a random book of mug shots. There was a bit of desultory flipping, but it was now late evening, and Milcray had just undergone major surgery in which a pair of steel pins were drilled into the bones in his hand—this at the end of a very eventful thirty-six hours. He was tired and in pain.

At some point in the questioning that followed, one of the detectives either did, or did not, tell Milcray that the body of Randolph Cuffee had been discovered at 103 Corlears Street. The detectives would remember this detail differently. Either way, Milcray announced the desire to make a statement, but said he wished to do so only to the male detective. Obligingly, the lead detective (a woman) left the room. Milcray then received his *Miranda* warnings, first orally, then in writing, on a sheet he signed. As Milcray perused this document, the male detective exited the room and conferred with his superior, who had been looking on through the mirror.

"He's going to give it up," he said to her, and went back into the room.

She stepped out to call the district attorney's office.

Milcray told the following story.

Leaving work for his meal break on the evening of the 1st, Milcray claimed to have taken a walk west, toward the Staples store on Union Square. On the street there he met a long-haired black woman who addressed him flirtatiously, saying as she passed, "You're sexy!" and asking him if he modeled.

He replied: "Where's your man at?"

She introduced herself as Veronique, and gave him her number and her address, inviting him to come by her West Village apartment around midnight, when he got off work.

At 11:55 p.m. Milcray punched out of work and made his way across town, into a neighborhood that, according to his statement, he had never before visited. He got lost, made a call to her apartment from a pay phone, received further instructions, and found his way.

Veronique, wearing a short robe, greeted him at the door of apartment one, 103 Corlears, and invited him in. The only light in the room came from the television, which she tuned to an erotic channel. For some period they sat beside each other on the futon, chatting, and then she invited him to take off his clothing, spreading a blanket in the narrow space between the futon and the low coffee table against the wall on the other side of the room, behind the entrance door. He reclined there and undressed, while Veronique stood at the edge of the blanket, at his feet, between Milcray and the door. Looking up, naked except for his socks, Milcray allegedly watched her open her robe, remove her shirt, and lower her panties. At which point he saw that she had a penis.

He cried out, "What the fuck is this?" and "I'm outta here!," to which Veronique replied, "Once it gets in, it's not gonna hurt." Milcray scrambled for his clothes while Veronique turned and put on a condom. She thrust Milcray to the floor on his back and lowered herself between his thighs. He, by this time, had managed to get his overalls partially on (up, he recalled, but he was uncertain if he had managed to fasten the bib). Bearing down on him, face to face, Veronique repeated her promise ("Once it gets in . . .") and began working to raise his legs and strip him.

At this point, Milcray explained, he went for his knife, opened it, and stabbed Veronique once in the chest. She, he asserted, did not relent, but bore down still more furiously and squeezed him to her body. He responded by reaching around with his right arm, over her back, in order to "hit him a few times," eventually slipping out of the weakening grasp, putting on his shoes, grabbing up his bag and jacket, and escaping.

In the street, he saw the extent of his hand injury, and the amount of blood on his white tee shirt. He ditched the latter, and dropped the knife, open, into a storm sewer at the corner of Christopher Street, before proceeding along that sidewalk and soliciting help from several shopkeepers and bystanders.

Sheepishly, he admitted that the tale of the five white males had been an invention, asserting that he had lied out of fear.

Milcray communicated this story to the detective orally, who then arranged for him to write the basic outline on a sheet of lined paper. While he did so (slowly, since his right hand was largely immobilized), the lead detective arranged for an assistant DA to come and videotape the statement, though it was now nearly midnight. She and the other detective reviewed the written statement and asked Milcray to add the location of the jettisoned weapon, so he drew a line from the mention of the knife in the body of the text, along the side of the page, to the bottom, where he put in a footnote: "in a rain-gate."

The video team arrived and set up, as did the assistant DA, who then conducted a forty-five-minute recorded interview with the suspect. This was later entered into evidence. In response to the ADA's probing, Milcray expanded on certain crucial moments in his account: Where was the sheet of paper with the address and the phone number? Lost. How close did he and Veronique sit on the futon? Close enough to touch, but not touching. Did Veronique threaten to kill him? No. Did Veronique have a weapon? No. Did Veronique ever punch or kick him? No. Was Veronique dead when he left? Milcray said no, that his assailant was still moving. Did Veronique look seriously injured? Yes.

He was made to rehearse the most minute details of the physical confrontation several times, and this made for certain ambiguities. How exactly did Milcray manage to dress while under attack? Did he try to rise? How many times? Repeatedly revisited, some of this became muddled. More muddled than any complicated story would become under close examination? Difficult to say.

At trial, the prosecutor—rumpled, gesticulating, deferential with the judge to the point of sycophancy—made much of the defendant's changing stories: first five white men and a melee (each time the prosecutor said the phrase "five white males," his voice oozed sarcasm, as if to whisper, "See how he played the race card, the skunk!"); then, once he was cornered by the authorities, a tall tale of a drag rapist. And even that story had changed.

Milcray's lawyer, in his opening statement, declared that his client still stood by much of the story he told the detectives, but that he now admitted to fibbing a bit there as well. In particular, Milcray now asserted he had not met Veronique on the street on August 1 but, rather, via a telephone chat service the same day. The defense attorney explained: Milcray had made up the story about the street encounter because he was embarrassed about having used a "date-line" phone service, and having gone to the home of someone he met that way. Milcray had a fiancée, after all.

The prosecution scorned this "correction" as bald strategizing, necessitated by the improbability of the first story: Who, after seeing photos of Randolph Cuffee (or, rather, of his somewhat distended corpse), would believe that anyone could, in broad daylight, mistake this large-featured, robust man for a woman, wig or no?

The defense attorney wanted to know if anyone had a photograph of Cuffee alive. No one, apparently, did.

Or no one willing to help the defense, anyway.

We watched the grainy color video of Milcray's confessional statement on a television wheeled up beside the witness stand. After some back and forth between the judge and a court officer, the lights were dimmed; it proved impossible to lower the shades, despite several attempts. The gallery had filled in for the showing—various clerks, assistants, a visiting class from John Jay College of Criminal Justice.

A large cockroach emerged from under the prosecution's table, creating a minor disruption. It escaped the stomp of a squeamish female guard, and wedged itself into an invisible crevice at the foot of the bench.

The taped statement was compelling. It made the evening of the killing feel close. The ADA was young, handsome, Asian, wearing a tie. He had a three-ring binder open in front of him, and he and Milcray sat across from each other, a narrow table between them, like tournament chess players. Shortly after the recording began, the invisible camera-operator tightened the frame on Milcray, and the ADA became a disembodied voice, inquisitive, measured. A digital readout of the time (both elapsed and local) rolled along at the bottom of the screen. One sensed that each question, seemingly straightforward, concealed complex structures: legal implications, potential charges, due-process considerations. The ADA took his time, making it clear he had to think before he spoke. Milcray responded quickly, telling the story, his intonation rising restlessly at the end of each phrase, as if he were looking for some confirmation from his inquisitor, as if he himself were asking question after question, in an eager tumble. The difference in pace, in caution, stood out.

Earlier in the week, on the second day of the prosecution's case, the supporting detective had taken the stand. The defense attorney, on cross-examination, pressed him to explain how he had gotten Milcray to "give it up" in that windowless room.

Again and again the detective said only, "All I told him was, 'Tell me what happened . . . just tell me what happened.' "

"Nothing else?"

"No. All I said was, 'Tell me what happened, just tell me the story.' "

But now, watching the video, one sees how grossly these seemingly neutral promptings distorted what the state really wanted: a "story" hangs together, is treated whole. But once you tell your story into the law, it becomes the object of a precise semantic dissection. The whole of the story is of no interest; instead, patient surgeons of language wait and watch, snip and assay, looking for certain phrases, certain words. Particular locutions trip particular legal switches, and set a heavy machine in motion. Milcray knew nothing of this, but already it was happening as he spoke.

On he went, explaining, the sound from the television speaker tinny, hollow—bottled like the little room itself.

Asked to show how he had handled the knife, he obliges, raising his right arm (in a cast) and supporting it with his left at the elbow, through the sling. He mimes an overhand grip and makes small, apologetic pecking gestures.

Pronouncing final "s" sounds, he has a lisp that seems nearly a hiss; he puts his mouth around words in haste, gobbling them.

"Yessir," he replies, often.

When he quotes himself as having blurted out, "What the fuck is this?," he excuses himself for his language, quickly, instinctively, in a whisper.

By the end of the tape, he is holding his bandaged right arm and wincing; he sucks air through his teeth in pain. Asked if he wishes to add anything to his statement, he responds, reasonably, "What's going to happen next?" And then adds, "Can I go home tonight?"

The assistant DA pauses, and repeats his question: Does Milcray wish to add anything to his statement at this time?

He declines.

The high contrast of the image renders his face nearly featureless, makes him a silhouette.

4. The Evidence

A day of warm weather comes as a surprise; the sun is bright, slanting over the top of the strange, windowless AT&T building that stands near the court. Things are wet, but they sparkle—the asphalt, the granite sidewalks, the dusting of broken glass in the gutters. Taking off my coat, holding my bag between my knees, I think how different the city feels in the sweltering of summer, now a distant memory: for months everyone has been bundled up, covered with many layers, no skin touching the air or available to the eyes. In August, though, in the Village—I am remembering the bare legs and arms.

How much more vulnerable to a knife, a body in the summer.

I walk up Mercer Street, stepping over a sheet of ice spreading glacierlike from a leaky downspout in the shade. Surely my heavy coat would slow down a blade, offer some protection?

I think about that for a moment, wondering what it would

feel like to have something partially in one's body and at the same time partially outside; what it would feel like to hold such a thing with one's hands. This thought (tactile, intimate) had preoccupied me long before I found myself in Part 24, though in the courtroom it has passed through my head many times a day. Years earlier, after being struck by a particularly gruesome bit of the *Iliad* (a lance to the lower gut), I had written a short poem, a limping sapphic, about such wounds—about being able to grasp at a shaft piercing the body, about the strange and sudden tangibility of one's insides under such conditions.

I was about Milcray's age at the time, amorous, hungry, prone to unreachable sadness and (I thought) unspeakable desires. The short poem tried to say all this. When I gave it to a woman to read, she said it seemed to her very much about being a boy rather than a girl. Maybe. I wasn't so sure. I took up fencing.

Valentine's Day is approaching. The world feels beautiful; smells, if only for this brief moment in the early afternoon, of spring.

Why would people ever stab each other, in such a fine world as this?

The prosecution had a great deal of evidence, but most of it for things that the defendant did not dispute. There was, for instance, no shortage of recovered DNA samples, presented by a cordially poised and slightly didactical woman from the forensics laboratory, and these linked the bloods of the victim and the defendant. But this, obviously, was consistent with Milcray's account. More troubling was the presence of seminal proteins on a swab taken from the victim's penis, and this became all the more mysterious when no traces of semen could be found anywhere on either of the condoms recovered under Cuffee's body. Semen also turned up on Monte Milcray's gray cotton briefs, which he had left at the scene in his rushed exit. Nowhere did enough semen turn up for investigators to get a positive identification on its source, or to say how much time had passed since it was deposited.

In addition to this forensic evidence and a selection of objects from the crime scene (the wig, a kimono-cut paisley smoking robe, the blankets, several blood-dabbed chunks of concrete lifted from the sidewalk in front of the apartment, the condoms, the knife itself), the prosecution had Milcray's own statements, a large number of still photographs (of Cuffee's body at the scene and in the morgue, of the crime scene, of the victim's car, etc.), a crime-scene video, a set of phone records, and the testimony of law-enforcement personnel involved in different stages of the investigation.

Many of these men share a manly density, a mass. In my mind's eye I see one of them clearly—Anthony Bonatoni, a crime-scene investigator with the New York City Police Department. Walking into the courtroom, Anthony rolled his shoulders to settle his suit, and patted down the front. It hung on him uneasily, and his chest displayed the unlikely symmetry of an oil drum. He took his oath with the pointed "I do" of an uncomplicated man, seated himself as if at ease, and then tried unsuccessfully to button the neck of his shirt, already filled beyond capacity. Giving up, he tightened his tie. Mr. Mackelwee, the clerk, took his badge number.

Between replies, Anthony seemed to shut down, like something automated, his head slumping forward on his bull neck, and his broad shoulders encroaching on his visage. A little repetitive clenching of the muscles below his jaw indicated that he was in sleep mode—cognitively suspended, but ready to power up at the next question. There was a vulnerability about him here, in an arena where words would be the primary instrument of communication.

And yet this is too cruel, inadequate even as stereotype. For "Tony" Bonatoni offered the sympathetic imagination a warmer array of immediate associations: the image of the deeply earnest, somewhat oversized student reviewing a mediocre spelling exam, considering how to do better next time; the spirit of proms now past. One can conjure up the nuns of his youth, the coaches, the extra sprints after practice. Parochial schools in the outer boroughs create men like these, and they present a perfection not to be ignored, much less scorned. Would I be able to do his job? Not likely.

Tony was not alone. Other bulky officers took the stand, eyeing Milcray's attorney with a defensive anxiety. Asked to establish times, they used military notation with confidence. Explaining the finer points of their investigative work, they spoke in clipped and technical cadences, creating strange sentences like: "These are the samples which were selected by me with the swabbing of the suspected blood for the identification of the medical examiner's office upon the certification of the record reports by me, which I did."

They had manifestly been prepped to ensure friendly, direct eye-contact with the jury.

Prosecutor: "Officer, would you tell us about the procedure for handling these sample bags?"

Witness: "Sure." (Turning to face us, helpfully, a pedagogical mien) "After the swabbing of the potential samples of the presumed semen . . ."

But on cross-examination this odd loquacity collapsed.

Defense: "Did you happen to see if the bolt of the door split the frame when it came open?"

Witness: "I saw a door, and I went through."

Defense: "Thank you, Sergeant. No further questions, your honor."

The prosecution also had a very different set of witnesses, on whom a great portion of the state's case depended. Hector "Laverne" Hebreo (to whom I shall here refer as "Hector-Laverne") and Nahteesha Breen both testified that Milcray frequented the "Fem-Queen Stroll" on Ninth Avenue to ogle parading cross-dressers and drag prostitutes. Moreover, they claimed to have seen Milcray and Cuffee together on a number of occasions, a fact they explained with the surprising and damaging assertion that the victim and the defendant had been, for some time, lovers.

On top of this, Nahteesha, Hector-Laverne, and a third witness, Stevie Trevor, all placed Milcray in the victim's apartment sometime around 12:30 a.m. on the night of the killing.

As Antigua's friends, these three also gave a taste of the flamboyant community of fabulous gender-bending in which Randolph "Antigua" Cuffee moved. We had been prepared for some of this in the process of jury selection. In *voir dire* we had been told not only that the case would involve explicit discussions of homosexual activity, but also that we would need to weigh the testimony of drag performers, male prostitutes, and transvestites. Those unable to countenance such talk, or credit such witnesses, were asked to recuse themselves. No one did.

Perhaps we were somewhat overprepared: as the first few witnesses approached the stand—including the robust Tony Bonatoni himself—I was ready for anything. Could this be a drag act? It seemed unlikely. Maybe. In fact, at some point I probably found myself musing that nearly all the denizens of Part 24 were, under it all, other than they appeared.

The prosecution's three key witnesses did test one's intuitive sense of such things, each presenting a different riff on sexual nonconformity. Hector-Laverne had cinematic eyebrows, pencil-fine and arched like those of a Balinese beauty-mask. His lips continuously pursed, he pastiched every gesture of a certain impatient femininity: a physical sassiness in the head and hands, a sudden and tumbling manner of speech, a tendency to cock his head up voguishly and glance askance, with much eye-rolling and huffy aspiration.

Nahteesha presented another, if no less hyperbolic, character: that of the sultry femme fatale. Whereas Hector-Laverne was fussy in voice and movement, Nahteesha unfolded languorously, her long fingers extended by tapered talons, her diction and intonation smoldering like a young Lauren Bacall's. The judge, in parley with the prosecutor, alluded to Nahteesha as "she," and then excused himself hastily, but that seemed to be her preference. When asked to explain her occupation, she gave an R-rated encomium to the generosity of her "*wonderful* husband," followed by a flicker of lashes. More poised than either Hector-Laverne or Stevie (whose partial deafness and speech impediment slowed his responses), Nahteesha made a remarkable impression on the stand, witty and brutal.

She discomfited even the prosecutor, who seemed very anxious to set the rest of us at ease with his slightly unusual star witness. Then, leading her through the first part of her testimony, he inexplicably got tangled up, saying "vegetable," when he meant "vestibule." Under the edgy circumstances, it felt like a charged slip—off-color, redolent of tumescent, pendulous legumes. People sniggered. The prosecutor perspired.

Both Nahteesha and Hector-Laverne told roughly the same story: that they had made plans to go out with Antigua, as they called Cuffee, on the night of his death (it was Hector-Laverne's birthday); that they had gone together to his apartment after midnight and had rung his bell; that he had declined to accompany them just then but asked them to return; and that when they did so, after perhaps forty-five minutes, there was no answer. It was Nahteesha who claimed to have gone into the entryway of the building on the first visit and talked with Antigua at the door of his apartment. She asserted that he remained in the doorway, that he was wearing a robe (but no shirt or, "heaven forbid," wig), that he opened the door sufficiently to allow her to see a young black man (whom she identified as the defendant) sitting barechested on the futon, and that (from the sounds) she could tell that a pornographic video was playing on the television. It appeared to her, she added archly, that the young man on the couch had a satisfied, postcoital demeanor.

"What makes you say that, Ms. Breen?"

" 'Cause that's how my husband looks after we make love."

She rounded every vowel with slow pleasure.

Before encouraging Nahteesha and Hector-Laverne to return, Antigua reportedly said that "Monte" was inside, that he was behaving strangely, and that he (Cuffee) would try to "get rid of him" in order to be free for the rest of the evening.

On cross-examination, Nahteesha made short work of the defense. Attempting to undermine her portrayal of Antigua as "a gentle giant," the defense counsel pointedly raised the matter of the dildos, whips, and sadomasochistic imagery found in the apartment.

"Honey," Nahteesha drawled huskily, with a touch of impatience, "we *all* have whips."

Undaunted, the attorney pushed on, trying to ferret out what he took to be a troubling inconsistency in her testimony—namely, the assertion that Milcray frequently ogled fem-queens on Ninth Avenue. Why, then, would Milcray have been in a relationship with Antigua, who was, Nahteesha had insisted, very masculine and never appeared in drag? ("Now me, I want to look like Tyra Banks," she had informed us, "Antigua, he wanted to look like Tyson Beckford.")

It was an ill-advised tack: "Let me explain something to you," she replied acidly. "First, the boys start out with us girlfriends, because they can fool themselves. Then, they move on to a man . . . like . . . *you.*"

She gave him a long look.

Several people in the audience laughed hard enough that they had to be warned.

Hector-Laverne said he had seen Antigua in drag a few times but it was highly unusual. To Nahteesha's testimony on the events of the night of the killing he added several other recollections of Milcray, including a description of their having been introduced one evening outside the Watutsi Lounge, and another of the defendant's having made a pass at him inside that bar on a separate occasion, a solicitation Hector-Laverne reportedly rebuffed by protesting that Milcray was "with" Antigua. A squabble ensued, culminating in Hector-Laverne's asking the bartender to have Milcray removed, which, Hector-Laverne asserted, the barkeep did.

Strangely, however, Hector-Laverne remembered Monte Milcray being introduced as "Ali."

Hector-Laverne, fidgety in his silky black tee shirt, fared less well on cross. He was excitable, too quick to attempt clarification. Pressed to explain how he supported himself, he submitted that he was a hairdresser. Was he licensed?

"No, but I . . ."

The defense attorney cut him off: "Are you aware that it is *illegal* to practice as an unlicensed hairdresser in New York City?"

Hector-Laverne began another explanation.

With a trace of badgering: "Just answer the question, yes or no. . . ."

The prosecutor rose to object "to the tone."

Defense: "Judge, I withdraw the tone. Mr. Hebreo, let's continue. . . ."

But already he seemed shaken. There turned out to be a number of inconsistencies among his different statements: the one made initially to police, later testimony to the grand jury, and finally his testimony on the stand.

And I sat wondering: "Withdraw the tone? How?"

Hector-Laverne had previously reported only a single meeting with the defendant; now he recalled three or four. In an earlier statement he remembered the young man he met outside the Watutsi Lounge under a different name (curiously, "Mohammed"). His memory of the goings-on at the Watutsi on the night in question (relevant to establishing both the date and the time of different activities) was cloudy: a beauty pageant? a performance by the drag lip-sync artist Piccolo Rainbow? both? He contradicted his earlier statement about the moment he first learned the actual name of the suspect in the case, and, more significantly, got quite crossed up as to whether he had been shown photos of the defendant and the crime scene before he testified at the grand-jury hearing.

At this point the defense counsel went for the kill, raising his voice and asserting that all of Hector-Laverne's testimony had clearly been a vendetta, contrived to avenge his deceased friend, and that he had never, in fact, seen Monte Milcray before: Would Mr. or Miss Hebreo, "Laverne," Hector, now please acknowledge for the court that he (or she) had lied under oath?

Flustered but defiant, Hector-Laverne raised his voice back, trying to explain. The defense cut him off, insisting on a yes or a no. He began again, again was cut off, and into the rising voices came an objection from the prosecution. The judge silenced the tumult and addressed both the defense counsel and the witness in turn: counsel would please control his tone; turning to Hector-Laverne, the judge explained that he would have to answer the question.

There is an academic discipline, Queer Theory, that takes people like Hector-Laverne Hebreo and their milieu as a subject for sustained scholarly analysis. One might be skeptical. *The People* v. *Monte Milcray* cured me of such skepticism. When *Paris Is Burning* comes to the grave forum of a murder trial, the result is chewy and puzzling. The campiness takes on unexpected power, forcing surprising juxtapositions and genuinely subversive moments, all the things that the denizens of cultural-studies departments promise. This went beyond how funny the sergeant-at-arms looked graciously helping Nahteesha (in precarious stilettos) down from the witness box. Take, for instance, this moment in Hector-Laverne's testimony. On the proverbial ropes, Hector-Laverne Hebreo did not answer yes or no. Instead, he wheeled around to the judge—a dry and disagreeable man—and, furiously pumping a crossed leg, announced like a Southern belle catcalled in a roadhouse, "Judge, I am NOT gonna sit here and let him make a *clown* of me, and I am NOT gonna let him *yell* at me!"—an exclamation so fantastically heartfelt and queeny and downright weird that those who weren't slack-jawed in the court looked as if they were sucking a fistful of Sweetarts.

But even stranger was the judge's response. A sour bone, a humbug autocrat, the judge paused for a moment. A wry smile passed across his beadle lips.

"I," he said soothingly, and with more than a trace of gallantry, "I am not going to *let* him yell at you."

This was the judge who had browbeaten everyone who had spoken to him throughout the trial, who had been magnificently impolite at every opportunity. But Hector-Laverne managed to pull off a completely unexpected (and seditious) tweak, teasing this berobed codger into a bizarre transgression of heterosexual norms: the judge had become, for a moment, Hector-Laverne's white knight and protector. Disciplines have been founded on less juicy moments.

For all its drama, later witnesses further undermined Hector-Laverne's testimony. The bartender at the Watutsi, for instance, readily acknowledged being friendly with Hector-Laverne and Nahteesha, but denied ever having seen the defendant, much less having thrown him out of the bar.

Stevie Trevor—tall and gentle-seeming, wearing a red

sweatshirt embroidered with a large cartoon character (Wile E. Coyote)—told a story difficult to reconcile with that of Hector-Laverne and Nahteesha, with whom he was not close. He had left New York and moved to Jacksonville, Florida, after the killing, and expressed little enthusiasm for returning to the events of that evening. Gangly, somewhat childlike (if also affecting a boyishness), he seemed bashfully reluctant to offer his blue-movie narrative. Some of this was surely the anxiety of a young man with both hearing and speech difficulties in facing the public spectacle of a trial: his lilting voice resonated with the multiple harmonics of those who cannot hear their own words.

"Stevie, did you go to the Watutsi Lounge on the evening of August first?" the assistant prosecutor began, loudly and with exaggerated enunciation.

"Yes, I did," he replied, his large, open hand grazing the side of his head, the fingers arched back, as if to push his ear toward the questioner.

"And did you see Randolph Cuffee, 'Antigua,' there that night?"

"Yes."

"And did you talk with him?"

"Yes." He drew the word out like a tone to be sung.

"And did he ask you to do something?"

Stevie smiled coyly. "Yes, he *did*," came the answer, with a hint of scandal.

What Antigua allegedly asked Stevie to do was to turn a trick, back at Antigua's apartment. As it happened, Randolph Cuffee ran a small gay escort service on the side, and at times drew on his circle of acquaintances at the Watutsi to procure partners for men who solicited his services. This was not the first time that he had called on Stevie Trevor in such capacity; Stevie had been in and out of foster care for most of his youth and was no stranger to living rough downtown.

Trevor accepted the assignation, and later that night walked the two blocks to the familiar apartment, where he found Cuffee, the customer (a white man with a shaved head), and a young black man, who was seated on the couch. Asked if he now saw that black man in the court, Trevor nodded; asked to identify him, Trevor looked pointedly to his left, raised his right hand in the opposite direction, and let a tsk-tsking index finger fall on the defendant, to his far right. It was an odd moment, as if Stevie were telling the teacher on Milcray.

Stevie Trevor claimed never to have seen the man on the couch before, nor had he ever met the john. Accompanying the latter to the bathroom at the rear of the apartment, Stevie began to undress while the customer inhaled an intoxicating "popper" and stripped. Asked by the prosecutor what he understood was about to happen, Stevie replied that he expected the white man to perform oral sex on him, and then, he thought, the white man, more likely than not, would wish to be penetrated. To these ends Stevie manipulated himself in order to achieve an erection ("ejaculated myself," as he put it) and put on two condoms, provided by his client.

As he did so, however, the white man took out and charged a small glass crack pipe (later recovered at the scene) and began to smoke, offering it to Trevor. He declined, and reportedly became angry, saying that he did not meddle with crack. Disgusted by the incivility of the customer and the "arrogant" (i.e., nasty, offensive) smell of toasted cocaine now pervading the small bathroom, Trevor testified that he removed the condoms (here he gestured in such a way as to suggest that he did so by pinching them at the base with his thumb and forefinger and shucking them defiantly), and exited into the main room of the apartment, from which, after briefly explaining things to Cuffee, he took his leave.

This testimony placed the victim in a new light. Nahtee-sha and Hector-Laverne both vehemently denied that Cuffee ever pimped his acquaintances or ran an escort service, but the prosecution did not contest the evidence that he did—including business records found on the victim's home computer. Trevor's testimony, however, also threw a number of uncertainties into the case. The most obvious of these was the presence in the fatal apartment of a sex-starved, shaved-headed white male, high on crack, who was about to confront his pimp, and who never turned up in subsequent investigations. One did not need a hyperactive imagination to paint a considerable number of scenarios for how this volatile encounter (mediated, somehow, by Milcray?) might have been linked to Cuffee's violent death minutes later. The whole business also made more spooky Milcray's fleeting allusion, in the videotaped statement, to his having thought he heard the victim, as he slumped into the corner, mumble something about there being someone else in the apartment.

Was the john still in the bathroom during the alleged attempted rape? Did he, perhaps, duck out after Milcray had fled? If so, perhaps he could account for one of the lingering minor puzzles of the case: Milcray insisted that the television had been on when he exited (in fact, that it had provided the only light for the whole incident), but the police testified that they found the television off when they burst into the room the following afternoon. Leaving the bathroom, seeing the body and the partially open curtain, and surmising that the light from the television would reveal the corpse to anyone who peeked in the window, did the john turn the television off in order to give himself more time to get away from the scene he had stumbled on? And did he merely stumble on that scene, or was he involved in it in some other way?

Milcray, of course, had claimed simply that he did the stabbing alone, in self-defense. But, then again, he had clearly lied before.

Baroque plots percolated in the mind as Stevie Trevor stepped out of the box, willowy and tall, and made his way from the room. Later, in deliberations, I would realize that others, too, found themselves fascinated by the possibility of ever more tangled stories—conspiracies, missing persons, Milcray taking the fall to protect, say, one of these witnesses we had just heard. Who knew? Now, as I look back, some of the hypotheticals we entertained (however briefly) have about them a feverish and fantastical quality. Such are the perils of the imagination in a trial: the sense of drama goads one to raise the dramatic ante; to conceive of fantastic resolutions worthy of the setting, the cast, the deeds. But not only that. This sort of reasoning—compounding improbabilities, dreaming up still more intricate motivations and counterplots—has, I think, much to do with a deep, shared idea about the nature of truth and the means of reaching it: namely, a sense that getting to the bottom of things should be hard work, should be difficult, should lead through long and knotty webs. Philosophers may wield Ockham's cold razor in the pursuit of the true (cut out everything but the necessary), using it to slice the tangled bits of life to the floor, but most of us would rather set to work with another sort of epistemological tool, more labor-intensive, more creative, better able to work with those tangles. Ockham's knitting needles?

This is not necessarily bad. After all, the truth *is* usually hard-won, complicated, and time-intensive; or, at least, there are as many truths like this as there are simple ones. Once let loose in a jury, however, such a worthy veridical work ethic can lead to the collective construction of giant follies. Everyone wants to do all the work, resist anything that looks too easy. More than one case, I suspect, has been resolved— to the general perplexity of lawyers, judges, and observers— by the operation of this earnest principle in the jury room: take the long route to reach the truth; no shortcuts, no matter how obvious they seem.

For instance, what was I doing dreaming up scenarios based on evidence as slippery as a killer's elliptical recollection of his victim's last, gasping words? Surely this was thought setting off down a long and twisty route indeed, and probably a dead end.

Still, if, as he lost consciousness, Cuffee did in fact mumble something about the presence of someone else in the apartment, there was another person he might have meant. Matthew Pessel was a sharp-featured young man with curly hair and a nervous demeanor. He looked about thirty and had the warm brown complexion of an East Indian. On the stand he wore a loud, double-breasted acid-green suit and a solid shirt in taupe. He brushed his nose as he spoke. It had been he who escorted the police to the apartment on the afternoon of August 2. Though he denied having been at the apartment during the stabbing, he acknowledged that he had been there right before and right after; and he had intended to spend the night.

Pessel claimed to have made the victim's acquaintance several years earlier, at a restaurant in the Village, and explained that they had become friends. The younger man periodically stayed over at Cuffee's apartment, so convenient to the nightlife downtown. Pessel himself lived in Brooklyn with his fiancée. On the night in question, Pessel, who at the time worked in a midtown bank (he now claimed to "run my own Internet company"), had been forced to seek alternate accommodations because his fiancée's mother had shown up unexpectedly. He called Cuffee, who told him to feel free to crash. After watching a movie with his fiancée and her mother, Pessel testified, he called a car service, confirmed his imminent arrival with Cuffee by phone, and packed a hanging bag. He arrived at 103 Corlears after 11 p.m., where, he claimed, he found Cuffee in a somewhat excited state, explaining that he had a "date"; Pessel could change (he was still in a suit) and leave his bag, but then would need to clear out for a while. Pessel agreed, and testified that he went around the corner to a bar, where he had a beer and waited for more than an hour. At that point he called, got Cuffee's machine, and waited some more. After several more attempts, growing increasingly tired and frustrated, Pessel wandered back to the apartment (it was now after one), where he found the lights out and no one answering the bell. He waited on the stoop for some time, noticed a small puddle of blood there, waited some more, then finally departed, spending the night in his office.

When he had not heard from Cuffee by midmorning the following day, Pessel contacted the police, explaining that he was concerned and that he also had property he needed to recover from the apartment (his hanging bag). He met two officers at the Sixth Precinct that afternoon and escorted them to 103 Corlears, where the super had dutifully cleaned up the pool of blood. A trail of overlooked drips, however, led from the street to the body. Pessel was not permitted to remove his bag when police first examined the scene (or even to enter the room). He recovered it later, at which point he had several moments in the apartment.

The significance of this lay in what he might have done during those moments.

Pessel offered the prosecution very useful testimony on the troubling matter of the wig. This object amounted to good supporting evidence for Milcray's story of the drag seduction. But Pessel testified that he had seen the wig in the apartment on several earlier occasions, and that it was never worn—always simply shoved into a corner on the floor, the relic of some forgotten gag (indeed, the wig looked more like a dirty mop than a seductive hairdo when it was introduced to the court—matted and tangled with bits of rubbish).

The defense attorney would later claim that, after the body was removed, Pessel (or perhaps someone else) could have, intentionally or by accident, kicked the wig around, soiling it, and thereby undermining the defendant's story (by making it seem unlikely that the filthy wig could ever have served as an effective disguise). Surprisingly, crime-scene investigators did not initially take the wig into custody as evidence, so it lay around the heavily trafficked scene for more than twenty-four hours.

Casting various suspicions on Pessel was not difficult: he had an odd, agitated manner under examination, and vehemently insisted that he had no knowledge of the seamier side of Cuffee's Village life—no knowledge of the escort service, of the drag shows, or of the sexual paraphernalia and imagery Cuffee kept to hand. (The defense attorney's repeated requests for this material to be entered into evidence—

particularly a set of sadomasochistic photos reportedly found in the apartment—got him threatened with contempt, to which he replied by moving for a mistrial. Judge: "Motion denied.")

Pessel also insisted that he himself was straight. Given that the apartment had a single smallish futon serving as both couch and bed, and that sexually explicit photographs of naked black men were visible in several of the crime-scene photographs, parts of Pessel's story stretched credulity. More damaging was Nahteesha's later comment, entirely offhand, that Pessel had been Antigua's lover, and that Antigua had helped him struggle with his crack-cocaine habit.

I found myself spinning a tale in my head, taking the long route through heavy cover: "Maybe Pessel did it. . . ."

With the prosecution's own witnesses so adept at undermining each other's testimony (just reconciling the timing of all these comings and goings proved very difficult), the defense rested after calling only a few individuals to the stand. For evidence, the defense attorney depended heavily on the outgoing phone record of Milcray's employer, which showed that several calls to a popular citywide chat service had been placed around 8 p.m. on the evening of the 1st. The timing of these calls corresponded almost exactly with that of a call made to the same service from Randolph Cuffee's apartment on the same day. The records did not indicate the duration of any of the calls, so there was no way to be certain that the two callers had overlapped using the chat line. But the telephone logs, indicating that the calls had been initialized within minutes of each other, certainly offered strong corroboration of Milcray's (final) story, that he had met Cuffee in a telephone "chat room."

The prosecution countered that the phone chat service had a function enabling callers to establish semiprivate voice mailboxes, which could be used to leave messages for friends: Milcray and Cuffee must have been using this service to set their rendezvous and keep their relationship secret from Milcray's fiancée. By these lights (and the prosecution found the technical director of the telecom company and brought him up from Tucson to testify about the voice-mail option), the almost exact correlation in the timing of the calls was mere coincidence, since there was no reason for the message-leaver and the message-seeker to contact the service at the same moment. On balance, the evidence favored Milcray's account.

One other aspect of the telephone logs offered a very imperfect confirmation of a detail in Milcray's story. A record of incoming calls to Cuffee's phone on the night he died showed three attempts to contact him within the span of a minute at about 12:55 a.m.; all three calls originated from the same Manhattan number. Only the last one went through; there was no way to say if it was picked up by an answering machine or by a person. The actual location of the source phone could not be identified, leaving open the possibility that these log entries were a record of Milcray's alleged effort to contact "Veronique" from a pay phone several blocks north of her apartment (though Milcray never said anything about making three tries).

If those were not Milcray's calls, then he was lying again, since the records showed no other incoming calls to Cuffee's phone at any time in roughly the preceding hour.

However, given that the emergency call to 911 (reporting Milcray on Christopher Street seeking medical attention) came at about 1:10, the 12:55 calls to Cuffee's apartment could only have been Milcray's pay-phone inquiry if we assumed a hugely compressed time frame for all the events he described: we would need to believe that Milcray found his way to the apartment, chatted, undressed, fought, killed, and escaped, all in less than fifteen minutes.

Later, this would cause much gnashing of teeth in the jury room, and would lead, in fact, to a rather goofy effort to dramatize the whole of Milcray's narration in order to time it. The project had the feel of an acting exercise run at double speed, and even then it was tight.

Although the phone record could thus hardly stand as unqualified proof of a detail in Milcray's story (weren't the three calls in rapid succession more likely those placed by an impatient Matthew Pessel, waiting at the bar, trying to get Cuffee to pick up?), the defense attorney cleverly turned the very ambiguities of the evidence into an indictment of the prosecution. After all, the actual site of the phone from which the 12:55 calls came was never determined. Why could they not be traced? Because, as it happened, the originating number had been out of service for more than a year, and hence had dropped from the phone company's records. But why had there been no effort at the time of the original investigation to determine the provenance of the calls? This, the defense could legitimately claim, represented sloppy detective work at best, or perhaps an unwillingness to look for what might turn out to be exculpatory evidence.

Conspiracy paranoia? Not necessarily, particularly in the context of the highly selective evidentiary work done by police at the scene of the crime. On a series of cross-examinations, the defense repeatedly asked those who had searched the apartment if they had found any women's clothing. Again and again the answer was no. But a close look at the crime-scene photos suggested otherwise: a gauzy bit of white cloth over the back of a chair, a bright red garment bunched between the victim's legs, what looked very much like a pair of high heels under the coffee table, something else on the futon. None of these items had been collected, and none of the witnesses who investigated the crime scene could say what they were. Given that Milcray's story demanded that there be, at the very least, a large pair of panties in the room, it was surprising that closer attention had not been paid to these various articles. In addition, it was the assistant medical examiner, not the police, who turned up the whips (which were never taken into custody); similarly, a number of other items of sexual paraphernalia appeared to have been entirely passed over in the initial searches. The victim's caller-ID system, which might have contained crucial phone evidence, sat unchecked until a flood of later worry-calls (including those by Pessel) had displaced records from the night Cuffee died. It was clear that the crime-scene investigators liked stuff with blood on it; they got less excited about everything else.

The same went for the prosecution. The lead attorney followed the general directive that the jury was to be shown as much blood as possible. The photos were good, depicting the spray on the wall, the pooling in the small of the victim's back, but the veritable items, bedaubed with the veritable fluids, were still better. The lead prosecutor kept his assistant (younger, droopy-lidded, sporting a bristly mustache and close-cropped buzz) busy snapping on latex gloves to open the bundles of evidence, each item with its rust-colored streaks and speckles. Every envelope, bag, or piece of Saran wrap bore a unique evidence label, not the same as that of the evidence it contained; this caused long waits while, for instance, a witness extracted a stiffened condom from three bits of packing material, and each of these, for some reason, along with the condom itself, had to be read into the record and demarcated with a multiple-digit alphanumeric code. Mix-ups were not infrequent.

The forensics expert, asked to link samples to the labeled locations on the floor plan of the apartment, twice pointed— erroneously, but with great confidence—to the same spot.

Much posturing took place around each of the relic-like items, as the sergeant-at-arms and the witnesses, too, were obliged to don gloves and handle each piece, creating additional delays and cultivating an environment of medico-forensic gravity. Not to be outmaneuvered, the defense attorney one day slyly requested the judge's permission to examine several items on the evidence dolly. Then, nonchalantly, in his pearl-gray suit, he wandered over and picked through the pile of gore with his bare hands, as if to say, "Enough already with the fuss." One had to watch closely to see him subtly apply a rub-on antiseptic wash to his hands after returning to his place.

Some of the defense attorney's efforts to undermine the state's case were more overt, and less successful. Questioning the relevance of a sample of Cuffee's blood recovered from the lip of the letter slot in his door (and presumably dripped there by the defendant as he exited), the defense challenged the prosecution's expert forensics witness: "But you have no way of knowing how old that blood is, right? I mean, Cuffee might have cut his finger on that slot two weeks earlier, right?"

Hmm. Well, yes, but there was the small matter of the pint of blood on the adjacent wall. . . .

Just checking.

Defendants in murder trials seldom take the stand. They are under no obligation to do so, and a jury is instructed to make no inferences from their choices. For one thing, testifying generally means exposing any criminal record they might have, information that is otherwise rigorously withheld from the jury.

From the start of the trial, this careful court practice—separating the admissible "facts" of the case from inadmissible information about the "characters" involved—struck me as more than quixotic; it was downright perverse. Again and again I found myself sitting in court looking across at Milcray. Only he knew what had happened in apartment one, 103 Corlears Street. Without doubt, the actual truth existed in his mind and probably nowhere else in the spacious universe, with the possible exception of the mind of God. What we all wanted to know resided in an electrochemical array in Milcray's brain, in the gray matter where his memory flickered in live cells. The truth was therefore *in the room with us*, in our midst, in a physical form, almost tangible, but totally illegible—inside the well-shaped head of Monte Virginia Milcray.

Who was he? That was the inescapable question. Was he a person whose account I could believe? Had he already been arrested half a dozen times for shaking down gay men in the West Village? What could be more relevant to the case than that? Infuriatingly, we could learn this only if he chose to testify.

What about Cuffee? Who was he? We were being asked to believe that he resorted to physical violence in a ravenous sexual rage. Was he a person of whom such a thing could be thought? Information bearing directly on this question was essentially prohibited to us, by law.

Somehow, in the history of jurisprudence, these issues— who people were, what they had done in the past—had come to be thought of as different in kind from the "facts" of a case, different from blood on the wall and reams of phone-company records. How had this idea gotten going, when it was so counterintuitive? I was being asked to decide if a crime had occurred—in other words, if *someone* did *something* to *someone else.* How could the nature of either "someone" stand off-limits?

I looked at Milcray, and I saw a cipher.

That changed on the last day of testimony, when, with a shrug (after requesting, unsuccessfully, more time from the judge in order to contact a no-show witness), the defense attorney called Monte Virginia Milcray to the stand.

And he went, long-legged, lankier than I had expected (I realized I had not yet seen him stand up). He walked with the smooth gait of an athlete, took the oath, and sat.

By taking the stand, Milcray voluntarily settled the question of his criminal record. There wasn't much: some unspecified "participation" in a nonviolent robbery at the age of thirteen or fourteen. Since that time he had graduated from high school (where he had been something of a track star), and had attended Marine Corps boot camp, from which he had been dismissed after dislocating his shoulder in a boxing competition, aggravating an injury from his high-school days. After this Milcray appeared to have held several regular jobs, one retailing at a sporting-goods store in midtown, the other doing data entry for a medical-records company. He lived with his fiancée (who was pregnant at the time of his arrest, and had since borne him a child) and her mother.

In the end, the bulk of the defense case hung on these minutes of testimony. Without hesitation, even forcefully, Milcray told his story again: he insisted that he had acted in self-defense, that he had been the victim of a sexual charade. After briefly rehearsing this account under direct examination (where he seemed shy, but clear and calm), the defense turned him over to the prosecution for the cross.

One does not become a successful prosecutor without a strong sense of how to play such a moment. This prosecutor's tactics struck me as odd. He elected to use a badgering tone, and a sneeringly sarcastic mien. He dove in by accusing Milcray of being a perjurer, for having "lied on his application" to the Marines. But it appeared that this meant nothing more than that he had not alerted the Corps to his old shoulder injury. Since the military assesses its recruiters (at least in part) on the basis of how many bodies they sign up, one could well imagine that no one pressed him to disclose an overly detailed medical history on the forms.

Given a defendant apparently so benign—young and slight, well spoken, with a handsome dark face, and bright white in his almond eyes—the prosecutor's combative strategy ran the risk of a backfire. And this, I would say, is what happened: when Milcray maintained his composure, the prosecutor had no place to go but up, escalating his belligerence in hopes of cracking the defendant's stance. By the end, the prosecutor had pulled out all the stops and found himself furiously dramatizing the state's version of Cuffee's final moments as he lay helpless on his face, with Milcray poised above him repeatedly driving the knife into his head, neck, and back.

Acting all of this out a few feet from the witness stand, directly in front of the jury box, the murder weapon in his hand, the prosecutor again and again swung the open knife, rolling his head and shoulders into each exaggerated stroke as he growlingly challenged the witness to deny that this, in fact, was how Cuffee met his death.

"And didn't you then—like this!—stab him? And then—again!—like this? As he tried to crawl away? And—again!"

But the sensational dramatization—which the judge refused to interrupt, and which sent the victim's family howling from the room as several of the jurors squirmed in disgust—built to a crashingly flat climax.

To the blistering assertion that this was how it had happened, Milcray offered a simple answer.

"No."

If anything was going to shake him, one thought, it would have been that.

So egregious did I find the whole performance that, as Milcray returned to his seat—slightly hunched, as if afraid of bumping his head on something—I felt a deep desire to see the prosecutor lose the case. How did that whisper of a thought affect what followed? It is difficult to say.

Sentiment aside, the prosecution's case left a crucial question unaddressed: motive. It is true that the law did not require proof of a motive (in a second-degree-murder trial, only intent to kill must be shown, not the motivation for doing so). But a sane individual, asked to find an apparently mild-mannered person—one with no history of violent crime—guilty of a grotesquely cruel murder (twelve of the stab wounds fell in a small area in the back of the head), strongly wishes for at least a wisp of a rationale. When none can be offered, it is hard to resist entirely, as beyond doubt, a claim of self-defense.

On this matter the prosecution had very little. In summing up the state's case, the prosecutor again harped on a myriad of more and less grave inconsistencies in Milcray's defense—the changed stories, the implausible account of the many wounds to the back (how could they have been delivered while Cuffee was on top, given that they were all on the side *opposite* Milcray's knife hand?), the limited evidence of struggle in the small space (knickknacks still standing on the television, right next to a life-or-death thrash?)—and added to these some positively weird things that the prosecutor himself thought anomalous: for instance, why hadn't Cuffee and Milcray engaged in any foreplay before they began to disrobe? If, as Milcray testified, Cuffee's penis was flaccid when he first removed the panties, how could he have had an erection just moments later, when he turned back from putting on the condom? Such peeves told us more about the prosecutor's erotic universe (it seemed to me) than they did about Milcray's testimony. As for the concluding assertion—that we were looking at "the face of evil" when we surveyed the defendant—it seemed patently false to me, whatever may have happened in that room that night.

Clearly there were very serious problems with Milcray's account(s). Much of what he had told us was not credible. Yet, for all that, the prosecution could offer distressingly little in response to that powerful lingering question: Why? The best that the state could do was to paint a picture of Milcray as a spurned lover, and as a man torn apart by the "inner demons" of his sexual double life. That night, the prosecutor intimated, Milcray had sat on the futon longing for more than a quick lay, but Antigua wanted to have sex and move on. (Remember, Nahteesha said Antigua was going to get rid of him!) Looking away as he put on the condom, Cuffee probably made some offhand remark, and something in Monte "snapped"—turning back, Cuffee found the knife ready-drawn, and barely had time to throw up his hands (he had a small cut on the web between the thumb and index finger of his right hand) in a futile effort to block the sudden surprise blow to the heart.

The key bits of evidence for this scenario? In addition to the ostensible difficulty of opening the knife (demanding that Milcray prepare for the stabbing while Cuffee was looking away), the prosecutor returned to the mysterious double condoms on the floor. According to his closing argument, the odd semen tests (yes on the penis, no on the condoms) showed that Cuffee had gotten the condoms *out* but had not yet put them *on*—hence, he was stabbed in the midst of doing so.

But there was an obvious problem with this. Both condoms were fully unrolled, with one inside the other, indicating either that they were at some point both on a penis, or that Cuffee put on condoms like no one else in the world. What was the prosecutor thinking?

The last defense witness was the partner of the police officer who had testified for the prosecution about initially finding the body. He was asked only one substantive question: Who kicked in the door at apartment one, 103 Corlears? He answered emphatically that he had. Unfortunately, his partner had earlier claimed the honor for himself, with equal certainty. It was a tiny point, but an oddly powerful one: Could we trust anyone who had given evidence on anything?

I ride down in the balky, crowded elevator. I have become obsessed with alibis and think, continually, about whether, if everything depended on it, I could establish my whereabouts at different moments in the past, the content of fleeting conversations, the minute chronologies of a day or an evening. Most of daily life, I am realizing, construed as evidence, looks flimsy, suspicious, improbable, lacking adequate corroboration.

When the door opens on the floor below the courtroom, the defense attorney steps in. We have been repeatedly warned by the judge to have no interactions with counsel for either side. I keep my eyes dead in front of me.

"Hey, Ed," he says to someone in the back.

They strike up a conversation.

The defense attorney's new cocker-spaniel puppy has just been spayed.

"Yeah," he says solemnly, shaking his head, "I have got *one sick puppy* at home."

Out of the corner of my eye, I see him smile sympathetically.

Is he trying to influence me?

PART II

The Deliberations

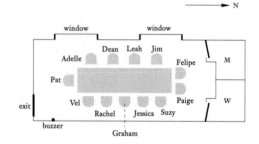

5. Into the Closed Room

Through all of this, through more than ten days of testimony and evidence, I walk to the court in the morning, go home for lunch (which I eat alone, reading *The Economist* at a small round table in a sunny corner), walk home in the evening. This strolling to and from my daily work brings me a great deal of pleasure.

By varying my route, I meander through SoHo, TriBeCa, Little Italy, or Chinatown, watching the life in each neighborhood: the giant geoduck clams, glumly clamped on their outlandish siphons, sitting in Styrofoam crates at the fish wholesaler on Lafayette; the porn-and-stereo-supply stores ratcheting open their metal grates on Canal early each morning; the impossible beauties sashaying along lower Broadway in the evenings. One morning I pause to watch a garbage truck smolder on White Street, abandoned by its crew, the flames beginning to appear between its armor plates, the sirens whining their approach. One afternoon I am brought up short in front of a Chinese restaurant called the Canal Fun Corp. There, in the window—in addition to the hanging ducks, their beaks charred, their necks question-marked by the wire roasting racks—sits a large clawed disk, like some grotesque crab. I look more closely: it is a pig's face, earless, and butterflied by the butcher in such a way that the split lower jaw spreads into two evil hemistichs of a smile.

Is this, I wonder, some sort of garnish?

These walks leave time for thought. We associate truth with knowledge, with seeing things fully and clearly, but it is more correct to say that access to truth always depends on a very precise admixture of knowledge and ignorance. This is nicely captured by the traditional figure of justice, a blind-folded woman holding a scale. With her balance she can assess certain things, with her eyes closed she cannot see certain other things. True justice depends as much on her blindness as on her ability to discern.

Where juries are concerned, the courts pay particular attention to ignorance: keeping the jury in the dark—about certain pieces of evidence deemed inadmissible, about the procedural technicalities that constrain the activities of the court, about the most basic sense of what is to be expected in the unfolding of a trial—clearly constitutes an important aspect of judicial practice. I assume different judges take this strategy to different lengths; and the spectrum of serviceable ignorance extends from sublime safeguards (juries must not be told that they can, in fact, disregard the law, or "nullify," with impunity) to considerably more prosaic obfuscation (refusing to tell a sequestered jury where they will be spending the night).

The judge of Part 24 liked his juries as out of it as possible. This became clear early—he was terse and elliptical when he addressed us, and had obviously given the officers of the court instructions to answer few questions and, when obliged, to do so in the least precise way—but this approach was never more in evidence than when he handed the case over to us for deliberation. He gave us almost no direction at all as to how we were to conduct ourselves in the jury room, and he ran through the charges we were to consider very briskly, despite their complexity.

These can be summed up as follows. We could find Milcray guilty of murder in the second degree or, failing that, of a lesser charge, manslaughter. The primary distinction between these was the issue of intent. In order to find someone guilty of murder in the second degree, it must be shown that the accused both intended to kill and did so. To find someone guilty of manslaughter, by contrast, it need only be shown that the defendant acted "recklessly" and in doing so occasioned death. Intent, we were told, was a state of mind, and it was therefore "invisible." How were we to make a decision about the state of the defendant's mind when we had been told that we were to constrain ourselves to the facts established by the evidence in the case, and were not to speculate or indulge in conjecture? Fear not: the law invited us to use our common sense to infer the state of the defendant's mind from whatever elements in the record lent themselves to such inferences. Another Gordian knot of philosophy cut nicely by the sword of justice: the inward states of other people were, in fact, accessible, for our purposes, by means of their outward actions. Next question.

This satisfying appeal to common sense, however, did not mean that we were beyond the realms of scholastic hair-splitting. For the prosecution wished us to consider the charge of second-degree murder under two different "theories": the standard "intent" theory, and another, introduced to us as the "depraved indifference" theory. I tried to concentrate with all my power as the judge enlarged on the distinction.

In general, he told us, the law had evolved to treat killing someone intentionally as more blameworthy, more grievous, than doing so without intent. However, there were deemed to be certain situations in which a person's action or behavior was so egregious, so heinous, so unjustifiable, that this distinction did not hold. In other words, if someone showed a "depraved indifference to human life" that resulted in a homicide, it was considered just as blameworthy as if the killing had been intentional. If we found that Milcray had acted with "depraved indifference to human life," then we were to disregard the issue of intent and find him guilty of murder in the second degree. If we could find no evidence of intent to kill but we did detect an indifference to human life that appeared to us no more than "reckless," then he was guilty of manslaughter, the lesser charge.

These were fine distinctions, the sort that Thomistic quibblers love. It was a great deal to digest orally, in a single sitting, without a pencil.

Nor was that all. The defendant in this case, the judge explained, had introduced the issue of "justification." Under New York State law, he went on, you can justifiably use deadly force if you reasonably believe that you are about to be the victim of a rape or a forcible sodomy (technical definition here: any part of the penis entering the mouth or anus). So, if we found that the defendant reasonably believed he was in imminent danger of such an assault, then actions he took that led to the death of the attacker could be justified; we were then to find the defendant not guilty.

Much of the first two days of our deliberations consisted of a sustained effort to understand the charges themselves, what they implied, and how we were to go about considering them. Some of this would have been easier if we had been able to see the judge's instructions, which he read aloud after the closing arguments. All we were given, however, was a sheet that listed the possible verdicts with key words for each: second-degree murder (intent); second-degree murder (depraved indifference); and manslaughter (reckless). We were also given a stack of ruled sheets for written communications with the court.

I say "we," but it was I who was given these papers, immediately before we were directed to leave our seats and file past the bench into the jury room to begin deliberations. Eight days into the trial, our grandfatherly foreman, Richard Chorst, had failed to show up.

Initially this occasioned only irritation. We had several times been delayed by late juror appearances, which kept us milling around in the hallway. But Chorst had been quite correct in all ways, sitting up straight, his suits pressed, chatting politely in a reserved, friendly, Midwestern manner, his hands perennially folded in his lap. Then he vanished. As his tardiness stretched past the morning, the court clerk made a series of phone calls, checking Chorst's home and, it was rumored, local hospitals and precincts. But nothing turned up. Out in the hall word passed around that Chorst had mentioned to one of us that he had a long-planned trip abroad that was rapidly approaching. Had he just gone AWOL? The judge wanted to wait, so he sent us out on our lunch break early. When there had been no word by midafternoon, we were called into the court, and the judge moved me to the foreman's seat, on my right, calling up an alternate to take my old place—Leah Tennent, the spirited young woman with the ready smile and global-village air. She seemed pleased and focused when she sat down next to me. It would have been very hard to have spent the weeks listening to the evidence only to be dismissed when the deliberations began— the fate of the three other alternates.

The judge made no real effort to explain to us what role the foreman was to play once the case was in our hands, and he never even made it clear if we were obliged to retain the foreman he appointed. In fact, the first thing I did upon our settling into the jury room (after proposing that we collect ourselves in several moments of silence) was to offer to cede my place to whomever we chose by a show of hands. At that early moment, when relief (that things were finally in our control) and excitement (something new!) were strong, people waved off the suggestion. It was clear several jurors thought that reaching a verdict was going to be a matter of minutes, so procedural questions seemed quaint, irrelevant.

I had sensed that there might be more resistance to my retaining the position. When I was originally placed in the foreman's seat, I rapidly revised my courtroom appearance. In place of roughneck urban wear, I began turning up in work clothes, the sort I would wear to the office: a tie, a sweater vest, a blazer. A few of the jurors remarked on the transformation, most in a cordial way, suggesting that perhaps I was trying now to fill the departed Chorst's well-polished shoes and keep up our collective jury dignity before the disagreeable judge. But Paige, the decorator with the downtown attitude, gave this an acid turn as we were waiting outside the courtroom.

"He thinks we are going to be impressed, and that this will help him lead us," she quipped to a few others.

Well, yes, actually, I suppose, there was probably a bit of that. But a bit, too, of simple respect for the forms, and, after all, I had worn a tie practically every day since grammar school. It wasn't that I was putting on airs, but that I had, in a way, shown up initially in a vacation disguise. At the same time, Paige was responding to something more than my suede waistcoat: she could read my general affect among fellow jurors as what it was, a species of aloofness. Over the first two weeks of the trial—in the halls, the snack shop, at shared lunches—most of the jurors had cultivated a basic sociability. Generally I had not engaged with the others, but had sat alone and read. Later, I staked out a small abandoned desk at one end of the hall, and used it to work on the index to my book. Paige, I could sense, didn't like the "I sit apart" routine, the "I read poetry on this bench down here during break" routine.

I could see her point. Academics cultivate a certain pomposity, most of them; I doubtless reflected years in that world. The resulting behaviors probably didn't really come across as particularly significant to some other jurors—to hardy Dean, say, the vacuum-cleaner repairman. Whether I read difficult modernist poems for fun in the hall appeared to be of no consequence to him. But Paige, as a décor person, had a sharp eye for styles and could scent the supercilious; she had seen college professors be jerks before. She was watching.

As a courtesy, I stepped out of my seat and let the others pass in front of me as we filed out of the box to leave the courtroom and begin deliberations. It was a formal gesture.

6. The First Day

Walking us down the hall and into the small jury room, the short, jovial sergeant said he would take care of us. "There's water there"—he nodded at a thermos—"and this is the buzzer you press if you need anything, and there's no smoking, of course. But there's windows in the bathroom. . . . That's all I'm saying, OK?

"Oh, and, uh, you know, if you order up the knife—right?—you know, I bring it in, but we don't leave it with you, see? . . . I gotta carry it around, and you can look at it, but nobody can talk till I leave. And the knife goes with me."

He gave us a kidding smile as he prepared to close the door. "You know, we need all twelve jurors for a verdict, eh?

"Anybody want cigarettes?"

Once we had collected ourselves, I proposed that we needed a few ground rules for talking with one another. I suggested that we speak in turn, that we indicate a desire to have the floor by a show of the hand, and that I would keep track of the order of speakers, so anyone who wished to contribute could. Everyone agreed, and almost everyone seemed eager to start to talk. I said I thought it would be best to begin systematically, by reviewing the charges together, so we were sure everyone had understood everything the judge explained, but several people complained that this was unnecessary and overly structured. I deferred, and we decided to go around the room and let everyone just say whatever he or she wanted as opening remarks. We started to my right, circling the long table: Jessica, Suzy, Paige, Felipe, Jim, Leah, Dean, Adelle, Pat, Vel, Rachel.

Immediately it became clear that there was nothing like consensus among us, that there was a great deal of confusion regarding the technicalities of the charges, and that people had significantly different abilities to think insightfully about the evidence. I remember distinctly the moment I realized what a range we were facing.

Rachel Patis, the kindly older Jamaican lady to my left, said in her opening words that she wanted to see the videotaped statement again, because she thought she remembered hearing Milcray refer to Veronique as a "he" at one point. This, she thought, blew the thing open: Milcray was lying. Hadn't he claimed that he thought Veronique was a woman?

Now, one might be optimistic about this: here was a close analysis of a portion of the record. But the reasoning it reflected was so wildly off-base (at the time the video was recorded, obviously, Milcray knew very well Veronique had been a man—supposing any of his overheated story was true—and so might easily have used either pronoun) that one was facing a very difficult combination: deeply limited analytical ability mixed with a Sherlockian desire to find the magic tidbit of evidence.

And Rachel was solid in comparison with Felipe Rodriguez (on whose finger, I now noticed for the first time, sat a bulky silver skull ring), who launched vigorously into an incoherent yarn about pig-killing in his native Mexico, a story that took an abrupt about-face and suddenly seemed to be about a former girlfriend, whose virtue he believed he had cause to lament.

"No!" he exclaimed sharply, suddenly, his eyes getting wide as he leaned forward and shook a finger at us. "It is true! I'm telling you!"

What was true was not clear.

Any prospect of a rapid verdict slipped from view as we rounded the room. Though there seemed to be something approaching consensus that Milcray was a liar, and that much of his story was false, few of us set great store by the witnesses for the prosecution either, and a slim majority appeared to feel that self-defense could not be ruled out.

More serious than the range of initial opinions, however, was the degree of confusion concerning how the charges were to be applied. Wacky new misunderstandings would emerge down the road, but right away tension arose around a single question: Did we have to reach a unanimous verdict on *one* of the possible criminal charges *before* we could even consider the question of self-defense?

This came up because people wanted to poll the jury right away, and so I proposed that we go around and ask if people felt Milcray had acted in self-defense or not—putting aside the issue of whether he was guilty of murder or manslaughter (and, if murder, which theory applied). We would have to sort all that out later, I said, if we were collectively inclined to convict, but why didn't we first find out who thought he was guilty of *something* and who was ready to let him walk? It was acknowledged, of course, that these first polls would be merely exploratory, and not binding.

Strong objections came from several directions. The issue of self-defense, a number of people asserted, was to be considered only at the end: first we all had to agree that the defendant was guilty of one of the charges.

The proposition surprised me; I could not understand how anyone got such an idea. I pressed, but those who spoke for this interpretation were energetic and a bit stubborn. Pat took the lead here. Raspy, blonde, buxom, she had the hard edges of a barmaid in a Back Bay Boston Irish pub; she also knew how to make herself heard, and took the floor without hesitation (not always in turn). It was early; all opinions had to be carefully respected. Consensus formed in the tacit silence of the majority.

There was no sense arguing about it. I proposed that we send our first question into the court, asking for a copy of the judge's instructions so we could sort this issue out. Even though I thought that the group's idea of how to proceed made no sense (how could someone who believed that the defendant had acted in self-defense *first* agree that he had acted, say, recklessly? what could be reckless about justifiably defending oneself?), I had a number of my own questions about different parts of the charges and their phrasing, so I was keen to examine the text more closely.

Everyone agreed, and I worded our first communication to the court, writing it on the lined sheet with my fountain pen (a fetish always to hand), which contained a foppish, tobacco-colored ink. It occurred to me that this might annoy the judge. After I read the question to the group for their approval, we rang the buzzer, and I gave the sheet to the sergeant who appeared at the door. Then we waited, and people chatted in groups.

Paige approached me and explained that she was very *intuitive*, and that she hated bureaucracy; she encouraged me to adopt a more freewheeling, less technically exacting (and time-consuming) style, both in the way I worded our questions to the court and in the way I conducted our discussions. This managed to come across as both callow and slightly condescending at the same time.

I said that it was important to be precise in writing, and not easy, and that there were certain exigencies constraining a group conversation; I would do what I could.

We waited a long time. We did not then understand that any time we sent a question through, the entire court had to reassemble, which meant going and getting the lawyers, the clerks, the reporter—in short, everyone, including the defendant. Reassembling the court took about forty minutes, and made it very difficult to keep focus and momentum in the deliberations: it was hard enough for us all to agree on what our question ought to be, and how it ought to be expressed; then, once we had reached consensus, it would be more than an hour before we were back together in the room trying to figure out how to interpret the answer.

In this first case the interpretation of the answer was quite easy. The answer was no. No, we could not have a copy of the jury instructions.

The judge said this clearly, after he read our question out loud to the court. Then he looked at me. "I can again read through those instructions. I want you to answer me, simply yes or no, nothing more: Do you wish me to read them again?" I said yes. And so again we sat through the whole thing, and then were promptly packed back into the jury room.

This, of course, had answered exactly none of our questions. We went back immediately to the issue of what question we ought to be addressing first. I did the best I could to explain that we should begin by considering the issue of self-defense. Our preliminary discussions suggested to me that there were about eight people in the room who were inclined to give credence to the self-defense claim (myself included), and that the others were divided among the various possible charges. Confusing the interpretation of this poll, however, was the fact that about half of those who had said they thought Milcray was acting in self-defense were also willing to say that he was guilty of one of the charges. Different people were confused to different degrees.

My own position on the case as a whole was somewhat flexible. I distinctly remember thinking, at the moment we crossed the courtroom to begin deliberating, how strange it was to have heard so much and yet not to have formulated a firm opinion. Not only was I undecided, I had no strong sense of how others would see things, though I did harbor an unjustified prejudice concerning Dean, the big workingman cowboy type: I thought it likely he would take the lead in pushing for a guilty verdict, if not a lynching. (I think I figured anyone wearing, apparently without irony, a large, cast belt buckle reading "Rodeo" had to be a law-and-order type, and quite possibly a bigot, too). Despite a strong distaste for the prosecutor and the judge, I had not yet made up my mind. To be fair, these antipathies, at least in part, proceeded from an ingrained bias in favor of defendants. Somewhere in my head, I knew this.

As we first went around the room, however, and I heard not only Dean but also six or seven others say they thought it *might* have been self-defense, I found my own inclination in that direction becoming stronger. Clearly, I wasn't just raving. At that point I pretty much made up my mind that I would not vote the defendant's guilt. At the same time, I did not feel at all good about the prospect of letting Milcray go free. I decided that I would just quietly hold my position and hope at least one other person held the opposing position, resulting in a hung jury. The thing I felt most strongly was that the case defied judgment on the evidence we had available. Was this a cop-out? Maybe.

When my turn came (last) to state my position, I demurred, reminding everyone that I had said at the beginning that no one had to say anything at this point. I said I wanted to wait, to listen.

The only person who looked a little suspicious about this reticence was Adelle, the other academic. She had immediately become the strongest and clearest voice for Milcray's guilt, under the most severe charge, and seemed a bit shocked that so many of the others were hesitating. Very smart and articulate, she was clearly accustomed to holding the attention of a room. Her aspect was serious, though not at all unfriendly. Dressed comfortably—in sneakers and a shapeless sweater with loose sleeves that she pushed above her elbows—she moved with a kind of force, often lifting her short brown hair off her temples and fixing it behind her ears, rubbing her chin thoughtfully as she listened to others. Because she gave all external indications of being temperamentally inclined to a pro-defendant position, her advocacy of a guilty verdict weighed heavily.

The time had come to make a decision about what ques-

tion we were going to consider first. Were we going to try to
agree on a charge, or were we going to begin by dealing with
the issue of self-defense? Logic demanded one answer: we
had to begin with the question of self-defense. Until (and
unless) everyone agreed that Milcray had *not* acted in self-
defense, there would be no way to reach consensus on a
given charge. I explained this, but the logic, for some reason,
failed to move several people. I would say that this was simply because they were confused. But Adelle also rejected the
argument, though she had to have understood that it made
perfect sense.

Her stance, however, was strategically sound. She saw, I
suspect, that if we first turned to the controlling issue of self-
defense, she would be in a substantial minority and her position would be put on the defensive. Of necessity, the talk
would turn to how she, and those who thought Milcray
guilty, might be folded into the majority. If, on the other
hand, she could get us going hashing out the charges themselves, this would surely shake things up: talk would be about
the stabbing and the details of Milcray's stories, and there
would be a much greater chance of pulling more jurors into
close consideration of the defendant's guilt. Adelle thus
aligned herself with those who were basically, to my mind,
muddled. It was interesting to watch such curious alliances
emerge.

I can't say whether she thought all this through consciously. Perhaps. But I sensed nothing Machiavellian in the
move. Adelle was operating in good faith; she wanted us to
make the right decision.

I proposed that we decide what question to consider first
with a show of hands. Could we agree to be ruled by the
opinion of the majority on this matter? Adelle objected. She

said she felt this matter was too fundamental to leave to a simple majority; we needed to be unanimous on it, as on the verdict itself.

And there we were, stuck. Should we vote on whether the question should be resolved by majority vote? Would we let a majority decide that question? I felt as if I were peeking into the origins of deliberative democracy—so *this* is where constitutions come from. . . .

Pat broke the deadlock. When she cut in (again a little loud, absolute), it became clear that we had even bigger confusions to deal with. She thought, she explained, that the self-defense justification was relevant only if we found Milcray guilty of manslaughter, the lesser charge. According to her, if we found Milcray guilty of murder, then the self-defense business fell out of consideration altogether.

In one sense it was a legitimate misunderstanding, reflecting the broader confusion about which question needed to be considered first: the truth was that, if we found Milcray properly *guilty* of any of the charges, the self-defense business was no longer relevant. The whole point of the self-defense justification was that it meant we did *not* find Milcray guilty of any of the charges. But people were mixed up about exactly this.

It was obviously time to send in some more questions. We hammered out a two-part inquiry for the court. First, could a finding of self-defense trump all the charges? Second, were we obliged to consider the charges and the issue of justification in the order the judge had presented them to us? This latter query, we hoped, would help us resolve the vexing question of how we were to begin.

By the time the court assembled and the judge read our communication, it was close to 8 p.m. on a Wednesday evening. We had been in the jury room for about four hours. The judge answered our questions succinctly: yes, and yes.

He then told us that we would be breaking off for the day, that the officers of the court would escort us to dinner and a hotel, and that we would resume our discussions at nine the following morning. There was an irritated sigh or two puffed in the jury box.

In accordance with the general protocol of keeping us hazy about what was going on, very little had been made of the possibility that our deliberations would last more than one day. The friendly sergeant-at-arms, dismissing us the previous evening, had advised that we bring a small over-night bag, perhaps a change of clothes, etc. But the eventuality of our using this stuff had been greatly played down.

I, however, had taken the hint seriously. Having no clear sense of the verdict myself, I saw little reason to think the process would be speedy. But I had other reasons, too, for my particularly close attention to the sergeant's suggestion: I am pretty obsessive about food. The prospect of having to eat for several days in crummy restaurants out near Kennedy Airport (there had been a rumor that this was where the court deposited juries) lit a fire under my preparations on the penultimate day of the trial phase.

That evening I packed my duffel bag as though I were going on safari: three pounds of nuts and dried fruit, three bags of sturdy raw vegetables, a dozen blood oranges, a dozen apples, a few avocados, a small block of Parmesan, and a round of country bread the size of a manhole cover. Tucked into an overnight satchel, these left no room for clothing. I barely squeezed in a fresh shirt.

When we collapsed back at the hotel that first night, which was indeed on the outskirts of JFK, these provisions gladdened my heart. Dinner had been a sit-down affair at an Italian place behind the court complex. The food looked better than I had expected, but I nibbled at the edges of things, and laid into an avocado-and-red-pepper sandwich once alone in my room. Mealtime conversation had ranged: I learned that the young woman named Suzy O'Mear (straight-haired, unpretentious, gentle) had spent a year in the Jesuit volunteer corps somewhere in California. She spoke of the experience with respect, but it had clearly been a rude awakening for a well-to-do Catholic girl from Sacred Heart College—homeless children and families, cycles of poverty and substance abuse, a cadre of off-puttingly pious zealots as co-workers. What had made the deepest impression on her, though, were the continuous con games played by the poor and the needy. Again and again, she explained, she had been taken in by the people she was trying to help, by their promises and stories, by the tricks they contrived to skim resources or broker sympathy; by the end, she said, her trust in people had been deeply eroded, and her sense that it ought to be possible to help others had largely evaporated.

I could sympathize with parts of her story. I had been the victim of a wonderfully precise confidence game as a boy, shortly after my parents moved the family to a marginal neighborhood in West Philadelphia. The material cost of the lesson had been low—a break-in, a few stolen items—but it had changed for good the way I thought about the stories people tell, particularly stories told to get my attention.

Suzy struck me as a very decent person, somewhat bruised by her experiment in social justice. We discussed how, for the powerless, narratives offer a potent way to draw new cards, to supplement the bad hands they have been dealt. These sorts of con games, I suggested, shouldn't be taken personally; they were always part of larger contexts of disenfran-chisement and social jostling. Suzy was not overly impressed by my somewhat mush-headed analysis, with its odor of piety and post-Marxian pathos. She was also strongly in favor of finding Milcray guilty on the most severe charge. She fig-ured she knew how to spot a liar.

Felipe, dropping his voice to a whisper, shared some unseemly confidences: The Jews, he assured us, ran every-thing in the Dominican Republic; they were wildly rich and powerful. "It's true!" he swore, to several uneasy faces.

The shower in my room didn't work; I took a sponge bath in the tub with a stiff washcloth, squatting at the tap.

7. The Second Day

Thursday morning, at the hotel's buffet breakfast, I sat next to Dean, who was manfully consuming a heaping plate of sausage and eggs. My own plate was empty, since I had eaten fruit and bread in my room. Conversation turned from my abstemious table habits to Vel's ubiquitous book on fasting, to the approach of Lent, to the love of God.

The more I talked to Dean, the more interesting he seemed. Not only, we were learning, was he a born-again Christian former crystal-meth addict (a habit he had picked up in the engine room of a navy aircraft carrier), but he was also a modern domestic missionary, who had been sent by his California "mother church" (of recovered addicts) as part of a small cell charged to found a new community in the drug-addled world of Spanish Harlem. Almost a decade had passed since this group had arrived (none of the faithful ever having seen New York City) and taken up residence in a communal apartment, living on resources pooled from odd jobs. No full-time work, because they needed to leave plenty of time for prayer, and for their mission: wandering in and out of the heroin galleries and the crack dens of the neighborhood, handing out literature, praising the Lord, preaching the possibility of recovery and redemption. They held their first meetings in an empty storefront, circling in prayer around vomiting addicts delirious from the struggle to go cold-turkey. The church now boasted well over one hundred families, and Dean had become one of its leaders, a deacon sometimes called upon to preach. He had married into the community, and he and his Guatemalan wife had two kids of their own; they were also raising Dean's daughter from a previous marriage—the mother's addiction had cost her first custody, then her life.

All this was by no means the *c.v.* I had imagined for Dean, but it explained much: his accommodating and gentle voice in our deliberations; his obvious ability to speak with authority and lead the group; his sympathy (contrary to my initial suspicions) for the defendant. From the beginning, Dean's attitude was that Milcray had done the wrong thing, that he had almost certainly gotten involved in something risky and stupid, but that this alone was not grounds for a conviction.

"The Lord knows," he would add, "I myself have been in the wrong place more than once."

One time the wrong place involved a horrendous van wreck (linked to a meth binge and a Hell's Angels syndicate) that had left him with an ax wound in the neck and a steel plate in his spine. He set off the metal detector at the court entrance.

Back in the jury room that morning, after a slow bus ride through the rush-hour traffic, we went over the meaning of the judge's answers. His having said that we had to consider the charges in order sealed most people's sense that we had to reach unanimity on a single charge before we could go on to think about the self-defense issue. I sensed that there was now no way to persuade everyone that this wouldn't work, but I made one more effort, explaining the way I would interpret the directive: what the judge said about "going in order" made sense, in that we could not consider whether the defendant had acted in self-defense unless we all concurred that he had killed Randolph Cuffee. In plenty of other cases, that basic question would itself be at issue. The rule that the charges had to be "considered in order" likely came out of such situations, when it was necessary to agree that the defendant had, in fact, killed the victim—in other words, that the state had the right guy—before even thinking about justification. In our case, I pointed out, there was no one in the room who didn't believe, beyond a reasonable doubt, that Monte Milcray wielded the knife that caused the death of Randolph Cuffee. Therefore, we could begin immediately to consider if his doing so was in self-defense.

No dice. The consensus was that the judge's instructions literally meant going in order, and this meant agreeing on a charge before we did anything else. I kicked myself for not having phrased the question more clearly. Adelle had prevailed.

She had also prevailed on the question of evidence. From the beginning she had made it clear that she wanted to start requesting different parts of what we had seen and heard over the previous two weeks: the pictures, the videos, the testimony of various witnesses. I had tried to hold this influx off. It seemed to me that it was going to be hard enough to keep order in the deliberations (already our basic ground rules of raised hands and speaking in turn had proved very difficult to maintain); the idea of the group's having anything like a successful conversation once we had videos and stacks of pictures and reams of paper to play with struck me as a fantasy.

But in it came. Initially we requested all the following: the crime-scene photos, the two videos (one of the scene and the other of Milcray's statement), all of the telephone records, and the testimonies of a handful of witnesses, particularly Nahteesha, Hector-Laverne, and Stevie.

We received everything but the testimonies. The judge called us back out and explained that the only way we could revisit the testimony of witnesses who took the stand was to specify the portion of the testimony we wished to hear, at which point the court reporter would search the transcripts, find the passage, and read it back to us as we sat in the jury box. This was clearly going to make it impractical to review the whole of these witnesses' testimonies (we would have had to sit for another week), but there would also be the difficulty of sorting out what specific bits we wanted to hear. How could we agree on what those were? If we really needed to hear them again, it was presumably because we weren't sure what had been said; but if this was the case, how were we to specify to the court exactly what part we wanted? This rule made a certain kind of close work with the witnesses' evidence impossible. For instance, a detailed collation of all the different times given by those who came in and out of the apartment the night of the killing—that was not going to happen.

Back in the jury room, the seminar-style conversation around the table broke open into loose groups gathered around different parts of the evidence: a cluster of people watched the television that had been rolled in to show the videos; another group circulated the photos of the scene and the body. I felt as though nothing could come of this anarchic room, loud with five or six conversations at a time, punctuated by laughter, some of the women periodically slipping into the adjoining ladies' room to smoke.

But I was wrong. Several interesting things emerged quite quickly. One of these came from the group gathered around the television, who had noticed, while watching the crime-scene video, that unless the door of the apartment was opened fully it was not actually possible to see the futon. This threw an important part of Nahteesha's testimony into question. How could she have seen the defendant on the couch, as she claimed, when she was in the hall and Cuffee was in the doorway? It didn't look to us as if that was possible.

This finding led to further talk about the three witnesses who placed Milcray at the scene. No one seemed to put much store in anything they had told us—too much inconsistency, too many indications that their "identifications" of the defendant had been made by means of a single photo (rather than a formal lineup or an array of mug shots), under the stressful conditions of a police station, shortly after learning of the death of their friend. Only Stevie Trevor insisted he had never been shown Milcray's picture by the police. But could his identification in the courtroom carry much weight? We had all been struck by what the defense attorney pointed out. The prosecutor had gone to great lengths to get Stevie, to bring him to New York, to put him up in a hotel and cover his expenses. This was a kid who had been in trouble with the police, on and off, his whole life, and now the DA's office has its hands all over him, and he knows he is supposed to make a key identification. Then he gets put on the stand and asked to point out the man he saw in the apartment that night. There is only one other young black man in the courtroom. It's not as if he is going to point to the wrong guy. (The defense attorney had played on this: when Stevie looked away and let his I'm-telling-teacher finger fall in the defendant's direction, Milcray's lawyer, sitting beside him, leaned back in his chair and threw up his hands— "You're not pointing at me, are you?" he called out in mock horror.)

On top of the somewhat contrived, DA-driven context for this positive ID, there was also the disturbing fact that Stevie's description of the man he saw in the apartment that night did not fit especially well with the way Milcray looked in his video testimony, recorded less than forty-eight hours later. Stevie (like Nahteesha) identified the person on the couch at the scene as having been clean-shaven, but Monte Milcray clearly had a fuzzy goatee in the video; Stevie described the man's hair as "nappy" (when asked to explain this term, he expanded on it as "peasy" and "rugged"), evidently meaning the hair was long enough to have shape, but Milcray's hair, in the video, was cropped to the skull.

The fatal blow to Stevie Trevor's testimony had been a clever trick played by the defense attorney, who presented him with a sheet of paper showing four police photos of black men, one of them that of Milcray at his arrest. Could Mr. Trevor identify anyone on the sheet? He puzzled for a moment, and it wasn't clear he had understood.

Did he recognize anyone in these pictures?

Hesitantly, he pointed to one of the random head shots.

He thought he might have seen that guy before.

It was not Milcray.

Stevie had probably just been confused, and thought he

was supposed to identify someone *other* than the defendant, but it certainly suggested that the witness could be led without great difficulty.

"No further questions," the defense attorney announced with a dismissive wave, and he walked away from the podium.

For all the cleverness of that move, the same attorney alienated a number of us in his closing argument, when he urged us to ignore the testimony of all three of the prosecution's more exotic eyewitnesses.

"I don't know how many of you have children," he began, "but if you do, I ask you: Would you trust Hector, or Nahteesha, or Stevie, with your children? If not, I ask you not to trust them with my client."

In the jury room this tactic was scorned as nothing more than a cheap effort to play on anti-gay bias. Still, we were gradually finding ourselves willing to put aside much of their testimony.

Or at least most of us were. Pat was energetically composing a list of all the testimony she felt she needed to hear read back, and the list was getting longer and longer. It included everything said by Nahteesha, Stevie, and Hector-Laverne—days' worth of material. And there was much more, too.

The other striking early discovery came from those who had been looking over the crime-scene photographs. In one of these there was something white and diaphanous on the edge of the futon near the body. There could be no doubt that, whatever it was, it had elastic gathers. In fact, if one had to guess, most likely one would have said that it was a large pair of women's panties. This created quite a stir, and the photo made the rounds among us. The only other possible explanation was that one of the crime-scene workers had left behind a white disposable medical hairnet. Given the quality of the image, it was ultimately impossible to say for sure (though I silently thought the latter more likely). Several people suggested that we request a magnifying glass.

We did, but our request was denied.

Still, a seed of doubt had been planted. The thing certainly could have been panties, and even if not, why had the object not been taken into police custody so that we could know what it was? Several of those initially inclined to convict expressed frustration that the police work had not been more thorough.

Pat, meanwhile, had assembled a list of just about every bit of testimony that we had heard over the previous two weeks, and she presented it to me, explaining that we needed to send a note requesting to hear all of this again. Bringing everyone back to the table, I encouraged us to think for a moment about whether we could start to put our fingers on a few crucial issues, the issues that might have the power to move us from our respective positions; this would help us hone down our requests for evidence. Pat preemptively objected, saying she needed everything she had listed.

But, I said, she had made her position quite clear—she believed that the prosecution had *not* proved, beyond a reasonable doubt, that Milcray had *not* been acting in self-defense. So she believed we should acquit. Was that right?

She said it was.

So then, I continued, perhaps we should ask someone who took a different position—say, Suzy—if hearing all of the testimony on the request list could possibly change her position. I showed Pat's list to Suzy O'Mear (the young woman with whom I spoke about volunteer work at dinner on the first night), who looked it over.

No, she replied, her sense of Milcray's guilt did not proceed from anything particular said by any of those witnesses.

I tried to use this to show Pat that it would be impractical, and probably fruitless, to place such a large request for material until we had figured out exactly what issues were decisive for people. Pat looked irritated, and stood her ground. She might drop one or two things, but most of it she herself had to hear.

At this point a few people seemed to be losing patience with Pat, so I shifted the topic. I proposed that we might try having those who were convinced beyond a reasonable doubt of Milcray's guilt tell us a bit about what they considered the "proof." That way the rest of us (by this point it had become clear that I was tipped against a conviction) could see what the key points were: perhaps we would be won over, or perhaps we could cast some reasonable doubts on those proofs.

Adelle objected to this formulation. Why, she asked, did the burden fall on those who believed him guilty? Why didn't we go around the room and have those who were prepared to acquit give their reasons?

Up to this moment, Adelle and I had spoken to each other relatively little. During the first weeks of the trial, we had chatted in the hall enough to learn that we shared academic interests, and that we were even in the same e-mail group for historians of exploration. We talked about a recent book in the field that we had both read. Quite quickly, though, we left off these topics. The trial seemed much more important, but we couldn't talk about it—jurors are strictly forbidden to discuss the proceedings before deliberations begin.

Once they did, Adelle was very vigorous, particularly during the interlude spent looking at the evidence—going from group to group, talking seriously in each, always asking questions of the others, her face lined with concern. For my part, I had grown increasingly certain that I was not going to be moved. But my desire to see a hung jury had also deepened, and Adelle looked like the best bet to hold down the opposing position. Suzy was more vehement, but Adelle seemed a more substantial figure in our discussions. The two or three others who continued to express a preference for a guilty verdict were much less solid: there was Paige Barri, the interior decorator, who had more than once voiced, with exasperation, a desire to get the whole business over with; and there was Jessica Pollero (of the bold knits and perfect skin), who came closest to showing disgust that so many of us were willing to let this guy off when he so clearly struck her as a liar ("I am so depressed by this," she announced). She found the prosecutor's "inner demon" argument entirely persuasive: the step from a somewhat confused sexual identity to a homicidal bloodbath did not seem to her like much of a stretch.

I replied to Adelle that those persuaded of Milcray's guilt ought to present their positions to the rest of us because that is how trials work: the burden of proof is on the state, not on the defendant, who has no obligation to explain himself. Therefore, those of us unpersuaded by the prosecution's case did not have to convince anyone of anything; we had to *be* convinced by someone who could adduce the proofs of guilt.

Adelle looked troubled. Her understanding, she explained, was that if the defendant was going to claim self-defense then he absolutely *did* have an obligation to prove, beyond a reasonable doubt, that he had acted in self-defense, just as the state had an obligation to prove, beyond a reasonable doubt, that he was guilty of criminal homicide.

This was not correct. Our instructions had been murky,

but I was certain that the judge had explained that a claim of self-defense expanded the scope of the prosecution's burden. In other words, the presumption of innocence extended to a presumption that individuals were telling the truth when they said they had defended themselves. When a defendant made that claim, the state was then obliged to prove, beyond a reasonable doubt, that the killing had *not* been in self-defense. This instruction had come couched in a few warnings: first, that in evaluating the testimony of all witnesses we were to consider what motivations they might have to lie (noting that this was particularly relevant in the case of the testimony of defendants themselves); and, second, that a "reasonable" doubt meant, among other things, a doubt motivated by "reasons."

Adelle was not convinced. I went around the room, and most people had understood things as I had: that the prosecution was required to prove not only that Milcray was guilty of the homicide, but also that he had *not* acted in self-defense, and that the burden of proof was the same for both of these elements.

Felipe got up and stared out the window, explaining that he had something he needed to do at three o'clock that afternoon, and that he sure hoped we could hurry up and get this over with.

One or two people thought this was funny; a number of people, including me, did not. I told him directly, raising my voice for the first time, that those kinds of remarks didn't belong in the discussion, that we were doing something too serious, that I was going to lose my temper.

He did not meet my look. The moment passed.

We needed confirmation from the court on the precise extent of the people's burden of proof. I began drafting the question. When Pat pressed me to include on the sheet a request for all the testimony she still wanted to hear, I discouraged her, explaining that we would do whatever we had to do before things were over, but that I could not yet make everyone sit through all of that material. I suggested to her that she try to edit it down.

After lunch (sandwiches delivered to the room; I slipped an apple surreptitiously from my bag and nibbled a fistful of almonds), we received our answer: yes, the state had to prove beyond a reasonable doubt that the defendant did not act in self-defense. We went back into deliberations.

Now we all had a common understanding of just how much the prosecution had to prove, but there appeared to be little change in anyone's position. Again it felt most natural to let the room splinter into smaller discussions. As I drifted in and out of these, I sensed that this format probably favored those seeking an acquittal, since each cell of the room's fragmented conversation formed around one advocate of Milcray's guilt, who confronted two or three skeptics.

People really wanted to focus on the fight itself. One group gathered around the television monitor, replaying over and over a three-minute segment of Milcray's statement in which he described the actual fisticuffs. Adelle took notes.

"There!" she declared, rewinding—first he said Veronique pushed him down twice, then it seemed he said three times! He had to be lying.

She scribbled away, building a list of the inconsistencies in the fight testimony.

Another small group focused on the photos of the body at the scene. There could be no doubt that, as the chief medical examiner pointed out, the stab wounds in the back formed very tight clusters: a rosette in the back of the skull, and two groupings along the spine, one at the neck and the other lower down. They were very clean punctures, showing no gashes or tears on the surface, and, according to the coroner's report, all about the same depth: two and a half inches, exactly the length of the blade in people's exhibit 7. The penetrating orientation of these wounds (which the medical examiner ascertained semi-scientifically by the methodical insertion of wooden tongue depressors into each aperture, using these to eyeball the axis of the incision, and then marking arrows on the body diagram that was entered into evidence) was basically in and down, not veering to either side. Only a pair of shallower scratches showed up on the body, both high on the left buttock, seemingly unrelated to everything else.

None of this looked terribly consistent with a struggle, or with the defendant's story that he had made the back wounds from under Cuffee, reaching around his body from the front. Moreover, the blood from the cuts had oozed down and made a little puddle in the smooth, deep recess at the small of the victim's muscular back. This strongly suggested that Cuffee had not moved much during or after the infliction of those injuries—which was also inconsistent with Milcray's story, since he had claimed that Cuffee continued to fight menacingly as he took the blows.

And then there was the matter of the blood on the wall, to the right of the fallen body. The prim, bespectacled forensics expert had smilingly assured us that those swabs of blood had tested positive for the DNA of, surprisingly, Monte Virginia Milcray. This meant that somehow Milcray had managed to spray a nontrivial amount of his *own* blood onto the wall between the TV and the window, some of it several feet high, some of it on the television itself.

There was only one way to explain that: the blood came from Milcray's severed pinky, and it almost certainly sprayed that way because Milcray was indeed kneeling over his victim in the corner, flailing away with big swings at a more or less immobile body. In fact, it seemed likely that he had injured his finger on one of the first of those swings, most probably one of those that landed on the back of Cuffee's head. These, the coroner's report stated, had not penetrated the skull (though they had made some gouges).

An excellent way to cut off your pinky is to drive a knife overhand into something so solid that the knife stops short but your hand keeps going. Something like a skull.

Several people began acting out the fight sequences as Milcray narrated them, trying to see if it was possible to imagine making the set of wounds we saw in the ways he described. Pat was on the floor on her back calling for someone to lie down between her legs. This and the subsequent wrangles occasioned a certain amount of joking, and I walked over to Dean, standing a little apart, and rolled my eyes: things seemed to be degenerating into a circus. We talked about the fight evidence together and agreed: it was not a very big deal that Milcray couldn't recall the precise sequence of the fight (after all, he would have been in a very heightened state); and it seemed likely to us that most, if not all, of the wounds to the back were delivered after Milcray had gotten out from underneath Cuffee—i.e., from behind— while Cuffee lay facedown or crawled, just as the prosecutor argued. It might still have been the heat of the moment, but the initial struggle was over by the time Milcray was in a position to deliver those blows.

"It's OK," Dean said quietly, nodding at the enthusiastic game of Twister warming up on the floor (people shouting out what Milcray was saying on the video, as couples wrapped themselves into unlikely positions), "this is good. Most people in here have never been in a fight—they need to see how it would work."

Minds did change in these re-enactments. Adelle was now ready to concede, when we again gathered around the table, that, contrary to her earlier thinking, Milcray's story of the hand-to-hand struggle contained nothing absolutely impossible. I pointed out that, though this might be so, it certainly seemed to me that the many wounds to the back had been delivered not as Milcray said but from above, after Cuffee was mostly immobilized, presumably from the first wound.

Didn't that mean I thought Milcray was lying?

I said it did.

Why, then, was I apparently willing to acquit, when I believed exactly what the prosecutor had claimed: that Milcray had knelt on Cuffee's back and stabbed him to death?

I answered that I was willing to ignore all of the wounds to the back. After all, none of them had anything to do with Cuffee's death: the chest wound took care of that. Anyway, there was no accounting for what one might do if one had just been attacked in the way that Milcray claimed.

"Think about it," Jim Lanes added in agreement. "Milcray knew he had to turn his back on Cuffee in order to open the door. Once you've stabbed somebody once, think of how afraid of them you are, think how you know they want to kill you. Don't you want to make absolutely sure they aren't going to come for you again?" Jim had abandoned his natty bow tie of the early days of the trial, and he looked slightly tired, gray. For someone in advertising he had proved surprisingly reserved, I thought, but there was a determined quality to him even in his silence.

Dean piped up that it was certainly true that in a rage one might do anything. He began to tell the story of his worst brawl in the navy. He had infuriated a smaller, younger superior, who leapt up from his desk and buried a ballpoint pen in Dean's neck while sinking his teeth into Dean's ear. He showed us the scar on his clavicle.

"And then," he went on, "I got my arm under his leg—because he had wrapped his legs around me—and I lifted him off, and I slammed him into this bookshelf, so he fell on the floor. I didn't even discover I had been stabbed until later. . . ."

"Wait," I said. "Go over that again. How did the guy get his legs around you?"

"He jumped up."

"But I thought you said he was at his desk?" I asked, beginning a mock cross-examination.

"He was."

"So you are saying that this guy pushed back from his desk, leapt at you from a sitting position, and got his mouth at the level of your ear?"

"Yeah, that's what happened."

"But this guy was shorter than you, right?"

"A lot shorter," Dean answered.

"And yet, in all the time it took him to do this, and to fly up at your face, you didn't even have time to move out of the way. . . ."

It was all an exercise, and Dean saw that immediately. It was a lesson in how hard it is to remember the precise details of a fight. We all trusted Dean, but it became clear that a hostile questioner could get someone quite tangled up about such a charged and impressionistic memory.

I explained I was not trying to suggest that Milcray had told us the truth about everything that happened in the room that night. Or even that he was absolutely telling the truth about anything. It seemed to me that the issue was this: Had the prosecution proved—beyond a reasonable doubt—that Milcray *could not* have been acting in self-defense? The answer to that, for me, was no. In fact, it was not clear to me that such a proof was even possible in this case: two men go into a closed room, one emerges, he claims to have acted in self-defense. How could it be proved beyond a reasonable doubt that this is a lie? Perhaps if the defendant had a long criminal record, perhaps if Milcray had been convicted on several occasions of assaulting gay men in the Village—but, barring that, I had doubts.

Jessica expressed irritation, saying that all this was ridiculous. At the start of the day, when I had suggested again that we begin with a moment of silence, she had said to me with a snip that she saw no need to do so. "I'm ready, actually," she declared. I had replied that this was excellent, that she could use the time to reflect on her readiness. Now she volunteered her complete agreement with the prosecutor's account: this guy had been torn apart by the demons of his double sex life. Milcray and Cuffee were clearly lovers, she asserted, and for some reason Milcray freaked out—because he was so disgusted with himself, or something.

Jim agreed that they had almost surely been lovers. "This is a kid who craved sex on the edge," he insisted.

Yet Jim was opposed to a conviction. Why? "Because it could have been self-defense; nobody's *proved* it wasn't self-defense."

Several other people agreed that it seemed likely that Milcray and Cuffee had been sexually involved, but that this alone did not offer clear proof of anything.

Vel had let her braids come down, and gathered them in a loose ponytail. I had gotten the sense that her unusual reading matter pointed to a wider interest in New Age spirituality: she had grown Zenlike in the deliberations, very controlled. Now she weighed in, serious, speaking clearly: she was not convinced by the prosecution. It was an authoritative tone, the tone of a manager.

"No means no," Pat announced sharply, riding the tide of opinion in the room. "Even if they just had oral sex and then Cuffee said he wanted more, if Monte said no, then it was rape." For this reason, the semen on Milcray's underwear, like that on Cuffee's body, meant nothing: although these samples strongly suggested there might have been consensual sexual contact, that in itself did not prove there had been no attempted rape.

Jessica rolled her eyes. Suzy sat back with her arms folded, slowly shaking her head. Paige sighed with exasperation.

Several of us said we agreed with Pat—that one could toss out almost the whole of Milcray's story; the only thing that mattered was that crucial moment. Did we have any proof that this moment didn't happen? Did we have any proof that Milcray did not say no at some point and that Cuffee did not reply with some sort of rough handling? Without such proof, how could we convict?

Adelle spoke. "But the only evidence for that moment is Monte's word, and what's that worth?"

She proposed an exercise: "Let's make a list of everything that Milcray has told us, and then let's cross off everything that has turned out to be a lie. What's left on the list?

Only that one moment. How can you be ready to let him walk out of here on the basis of that?"

Felipe piped up that we need not worry about Milcray's going free—even if we found him not guilty, he would go to jail for a good long time.

This drew a number of puzzled stares. Several of us tried to explain that this was incorrect, that if we found Milcray not guilty he would be released. Felipe looked unconvinced, but he did not argue.

Then a new idea started to circulate. Given such a strong division between those who thought Milcray was guilty of the highest charge (Suzy, Adelle) and those who thought he was absolutely not guilty of anything (Leah, Pat), wasn't the wisest thing, the most responsible and mature thing, to seek some sort of compromise? For instance, couldn't both extremes start to move toward some middle ground? Say, a conviction on the lesser charge of manslaughter?

This suggestion had a reasonable quality, and a few people (Felipe, possibly Rachel, probably others) were clearly willing to consider it. Paige pleaded for a negotiated settlement: "We can't be too rigid here—we have to try to work with each other."

Jessica agreed. Hadn't we all admitted that what Milcray did was very bad? After all, it was clear he had abandoned a man he knew to be horribly wounded. That alone deserved some sort of punishment. We couldn't just let him walk free when all of us agreed that he had done something quite terrible—terrible regardless of whether he thought, at first, that he was acting in self-defense.

I wanted to head off this kind of argument. "The problem with a compromise," I said, "is that it would be a violation of our duty as jurors, which is to apply the law. We weren't asked to consider whether Milcray is guilty of abandoning the scene or lying to police. The law says that we can only convict if we're persuaded, beyond a reasonable doubt, that Milcray killed Cuffee and did not do so in self-defense. So that's the only issue. We aren't allowed to fudge the law because we'd like to see Milcray get punished."

Pat spoke up: "Yeah, I'm angry that the police didn't do a better job, because if they had I might be able to convict, but the proof isn't there, and that's it."

There was a categorical quality to her every contribution.

Suzy and Paige both expressed irritation, but it was Adelle who spoke.

"But do we really have to apply the law? Who can make us? There is something called nullification—right?—where a jury disregards the law and does what it thinks is right?" She looked at me.

I nodded.

"What about that?" she asked.

I had been standing, and I sat down. "Sure, there is always that," I said. "Do you want to tell us more?"

We did a deferential two-step deciding who would give a brief history of nullification. It fell to me, so I told the story as best I remembered it from quizzing my wife for her legal-history exams: some famous English case from the seventeenth century; the jury acquitted when the defendant was obviously guilty, doing so as a protest against the law itself; the judge threw the jury in jail, to force them to reach the "correct" verdict; somehow the judge ended up getting censured and the jury was set free, unpunished. Result? A venerable precedent in our legal tradition: juries can do whatever they please, and they are immune from prosecution.

"If we want," I concluded, "we can ignore the law."

The plea for compromise gained renewed strength in light of this story. Paige heaped scorn on the pedantry of those who would allow themselves to be constrained by the "letter" of the law while ignoring its "spirit"—a spirit, she explained, that amounted to the righteous desire not to let people who do bad things go unpunished.

"We need a more *sensual* approach," she urged, moving her hands as if she were feeling the nap on a piece of upholstery. It seemed to me she did not mean the term literally, but that in downtown interior decorating "sensual" was probably used in a general way to mean "good" or "appropriate."

To exemplify this more nuanced approach, Paige conceded that by now she was convinced that the prosecution had failed: they had not proved beyond a reasonable doubt that Milcray hadn't acted in self-defense. And yet she still felt willing to find the defendant guilty of manslaughter, so that he would be punished for all the things he *had* done— lie, abandon the wounded man, etc. Who was prepared to join her?

I spoke up before anyone else had a chance and said that I, for one, would definitely not support such a verdict, so we could rule out ever achieving unanimity on such grounds. If someone persuaded me that Milcray was guilty of one of the charges, then I was prepared to convict, but I wasn't going to vote the defendant's guilt as part of some compromise. Moreover, if she now really had reasonable doubts about Milcray's actions, then duty obliged her to acquit.

Conversation heated up around the table, as people debated this idea of a compromise verdict. Several others said—for instance, Leah, quite passionately—they would never agree to convict Milcray using that rationale.

Jessica held up one of the photos of Cuffee's apartment.

High on the wall, she pointed out, opposite the door, hung a modest, sobering crucifix; it presided over the small room.

"All this talk about Milcray," she said, "Milcray this, Milcray that. What about Cuffee?"

By this point it was well into the evening, and people wanted to poll again, on each of the charges, in order, with the question of self-defense last. When we did, the results were all over the place. At first it seemed more jurors wanted to convict: two voted guilty on second-degree murder with intent, and another five or six voted guilty on either murder under the depraved-indifference clause or manslaughter. But then we counted the small, torn bits of paper that served as ballots on the issue of self-defense: one "no," eight "yes," and three "undecided." So, in fact, there had been a slight movement in the direction of an acquittal. But there remained sufficient confusion over the need to get consensus on a charge that it was hard to interpret the results.

The subject of a hung jury had hardly come up at all in our first two days, but in the silence that followed this count I offered it to the room as a possibility: "You know," I said, "we might just write the court a note, explaining that we have been doing the best we can for something like"—I looked at my watch—"fifteen hours, and that we feel like we are stuck."

"He'd just send us back to keep going," someone said.

"Yeah, what does he care . . ." Jim added.

"Well," I tried again, "juries do hang. I mean, I don't know what it takes before the judge gives up, but my sense is that things look pretty intractable in this room. After all this, we are still basically right where we were in the first minute of the first day. . . ."

Even as I started talking, I could see the pained expressions and the shaking heads. I was getting nowhere with this suggestion.

Leah cut me off: "Absolutely not. I think it's way too early to give up."

As discussions unfolded, she had become one of the most vehement voices in favor of an acquittal. In fact, she seemed to be the only person in the room genuinely willing to believe Milcray, and to credit his story. The other seven of us who opposed conviction to varying degrees generally agreed that if this were God's lottery, and we had to bet on whether Milcray had murdered Randolph Cuffee outright, the safe money would say he had. But that, we realized, was not the question. As Vel had pointed out earlier in the day, "Not guilty doesn't mean innocent."

Adelle was shaking her head and looking quite dismayed, but before she could say what she was thinking, Pat jumped in, very excited and upset. She was furious at me for even bringing up the idea of a hung jury. Hadn't she been asking me all day to turn in her request to hear a great deal of testimony again? What about all of that? Had I just been stringing her along the whole time, encouraging her to revise the list and edit it, when I had no intention of ever submitting the request? Where did I get off, talking about giving up when we hadn't even gone over the evidence that everyone wanted to hear?

This barrage set me aback. I had certainly stalled her request, because it seemed to me irrelevant to the proceedings, and because I didn't feel I could commit all twelve of us to the jury box for the next three or four days to review testimony that (as best I could make out) only one person wanted to hear—particularly when that one person insisted vociferously that she had entirely made up her mind about the whole case. My surprise was all the greater because I had made subtle efforts to cultivate good relations with those who were advocating acquittal, particularly those like Pat who were very vocal. I had tried to make her feel that I was her partner in the process, and that we were very much on the same side. Had this come across as condescending? Perhaps.

But there was something else, too. Increasingly Pat struck me as emotionally volatile. From her sudden, explosive inter-jections I had started to get the sense of someone quick to trigger. Added to this was the issue of her medication. She was apparently taking a heavily regulated prescription drug of some sort, and she was running low. Pressing the sergeant-at-arms for help in securing a refill earlier that morning, she had looked close to tears. She was going through packs of Kools in the bathroom at an alarming rate.

I apologized to Pat, but I tried to stand my ground, too, pointing out that I had a duty to think about the flow of our deliberations as a group, and to balance everyone's requests. In response, she grew more aggressive, not less, nearly shout-ing, accusing me of ignoring her, disrespecting her, and dis-regarding the work she had put in reviewing the evidence.

The woman knew how to fight, that was evident; she was obviously less clear on how to de-escalate a confrontation, and when it might be preferable to do so.

A loud bang sounded on the heavy door, and the bailiff's voice called: "Cease deliberations!" He put his head in: "Jurors, please assemble in the courtroom."

Time was up. Another overnight lay ahead.

The atmosphere had soured a great deal in the last few minutes. I was tired, and a little angry to have come under an attack that seemed to me slightly unhinged. Everyone was disappointed and irritated at having to spend another night in a lousy motel. There was a palpable sense of failure: we had not managed to reach a verdict.

A few people asked that we not be taken to dinner as a group but simply pick up pizzas and go to the hotel, allowing us all to eat alone in our rooms. The sergeant said no, and the other officers who were escorting us tried to tell us that everything would be OK, that we were just tired, and that we needed to get out of the jury room and settle down, talk about other things (outside the jury room we were prohibited from discussing the case). The truth is, we were good and sick of one another, but there was no choice—we had to eat together, court orders.

We headed to another small place near City Hall. Adelle approached me as I was gathering up my things and offered a few words of encouragement. "You're doing fine," she said kindly. I shrugged. I knew what I thought about what had happened: if anyone felt left out or screwed over in the process, it was my fault, because I was responsible for managing the room, managing the conversation, and managing the array of psyches around the table. I had erred in assessing Pat's situation. I would have to do better.

All the same, I longed to be alone, and the prospect of another sit-down dinner had all the appeal of a tooth extraction. I made my way to a table and sat. We were four: Dean, Jim, Jessica, and I. I ordered salmon and a green salad, but ate almost nothing.

The officers of the court sat together again, but they were making a special effort to be sweet to us. They had collected our phone messages with particular attention (we would write them on sheets of paper and they would make the calls to deliver them), and they tried a few jokes to break up the

gray mood that had sunk over us. My wife was out of the
United States, so they couldn't get the court phones to reach
her. One of the officers, a very tall and sturdy Hispanic
woman with a crew cut, took me into the back of the restaurant and let me dial at the pay phone using my calling card.
She held the receiver. "It's an answering machine," she whispered to me, and then began to speak: "This is Sergeant
Gainez of New York Supreme Court Criminal Division, and
I have a message here . . ." and she held the receiver out to
me. I told my wife I loved her, without touching the phone,
and then Sergeant Gainez hung it back up. She put her finger to her lips as she turned back to me. That little breach of
the regulations was our secret.

I went back to the table in a better mood. Putting the trial
behind us had a curiously intoxicating effect. Conversation
warmed. We talked about our jobs: Dean got into Madison
Square Garden free for Rangers games because he repaired
the building's giant ride-on vacuum cleaners. Jim asked me
about the stack of papers I had always toted around during
the trial, and that led to questions about my book, about the
life of academics. I described the courses I had taught lately,
and explained how I had gotten interested in the history
of science. Unlike conversations in university settings—
where, too often, one feels compelled to affect familiarity
with whatever subject comes up (an occupational hazard
of being "professionally" knowledgeable)—Jessica, Jim, and
Dean actually expressed curiosity: the idea that somebody
could spend six years studying the work of a handful of
Amerindians and geographical explorers somewhere in South
America more than a century ago struck them as so entirely
quixotic, so idiosyncratic and outlandish, that their questions
reminded me of the subject's romance, something I had

largely forgotten five and a half years earlier. They all wanted to read the book; I said that it had footnotes, and it was not going to be a best-seller. They stuck to their guns: they'd be watching Amazon.com.

The world somehow seemed large again. For us, in the last weeks, it had mostly contracted to a few hours one August night more than a year earlier; but the stories of shamans ogling a Schmalcalder compass on the Takutu in 1842 had reminded us that there was more to life than the pattern of incisions in Cuffee's back.

Dean, a bit giddy from the weirdness of the whole thing, made a confession: "You know, you can't ever judge people by how they look. I've got to tell you," he said, turning to me, "that you are not at all like what I thought when I saw you at first."

I was pretty sure I knew what he meant, but I asked.

"Well," he said, "you were wearing work boots and those red sweatpants every day, you never shaved, you were always stretching out and doing weird exercises in the hall—I just figured . . . Well, I wouldn't ever have guessed that you had a Ph.D."

I could say something similar to him, and I did: "Truth is, I had you sized up totally differently, too—I saw you dipping chaw in the hall, with your cowboy boots and your tattoo, and you seemed like a pretty conservative good-ol'-boy type to me, and then I find out you're nothing like that."

"It goes to show you," he said, nodding.

The mood had gone from glum to something almost misty-eyed. Pretty soon we'd be having an Iron John moment; I was as much caught up in it as the others.

Why *was* I stretching all the time? somebody asked. I said

I had a bum leg from a sports injury and it cramped up on me. This led to the story of what had happened on one of the first days of the trial, when the judge pointedly asked me to remain in my seat after he dismissed the other jurors for the evening. What had that been about? I explained that the judge had given me a dressing-down for having stood up to stretch twice during brief pauses in the day of testimony. I recounted how I had tried to explain to him that I had, each time, asked permission from the sergeant-at-arms who sat beside us, and that each time he had said it was not a problem. But the judge shouted me down, threatened to throw me off the jury, upbraided me for having failed to alert the court that I was unfit for service, and scolded me for disregarding the seriousness of the office. All this in front of the full and open court. Then he summarily sent me from the room. The poor sergeant approached me later to say that I shouldn't worry about it (looking closely, we could sometimes catch the court officers in shared moments of insubordinate mockery of the judge, under his very nose), but of course I was furious and humiliated, as well as anxious that I would be replaced by one of the alternates and sent home.

Jessica said the judge was the rudest person she had ever met, and Jim shook his head in disgust. I said, in the end, it had all been for the good: I had been forced to practice sitting still all day, and this had obliged me to concentrate on keeping the leg relaxed. I had learned I had much more control over the discomfort than I ever knew—it had been a matter of meditative discipline, of refusing to let the cramps get going, because then they only got worse.

Dean had the workingman's impulse to collective action. He proposed that if I ever again needed to stand up in the jury box I should let him know, and he would see to it that the whole jury stood up for as long as I needed. He was too pious a man to say, "Fuck the judge."

It was an intoxicating moment, a moment of solidarity—that of the table, and of the jury as a whole. On the bus ride out to La Guardia (a different airport, a different hotel), Dean and I sat together in the back, in the soothing dark, bumped by the potholes, and he told the story of riding out an engine-room fire on an aircraft carrier in the Persian Gulf.

This trial was not the first time Dean had been adrift, locked in a small, hot room with a dozen angry people.

Our crucible was Friday.

8. The Third Day

For the third time we start with ten seconds of silence, and then I request a moment to speak. I begin by apologizing, sincerely and carefully, to Pat, for having hurt her feelings. I ask her to forgive me, and to be patient; I am doing the best I can. She nods. Then I say a few words of encouragement, pointing out again what a difficult thing we have been doing together, spending more than a dozen hours in sustained conversation about such a grave matter. Already this is no small achievement. I tell them that I have been deeply impressed by their hard work, and that they ought to congratulate themselves.

All this was only partially true. It would have been more correct to say that I had been quite disgusted by several of the participants—so alienated by Felipe, in particular, by what I viewed as his incontinent ramblings, by his seemingly total disregard for the significance of the matter at hand, that the previous evening, lying on top of the bedspread in the green-brown hotel room, I had written a grim assessment in my notebook:

> At several moments I have felt that my refusal to accord with a guilty verdict will reflect as much [as anything else] a rejection of the competency of this body of jurors to reflect weightily on a matter of such seriousness. In different circumstances I can imagine having a certain kind of conversation that could bring me around to reject the justification of self-defense. But there are some jurors here who are such idiots, so thoroughly oblivious to good judgment, or so thick (regardless of their intentions), that it seems improper to aid them in depriving a man of his liberty.

This was what I had actually been thinking. But pointing it out seemed unlikely to raise the tone of our discourse.

To placate Pat, I requested from the group a special dispensation: that before we got under way she be permitted to take as much time as she needed to frame for us what she thought were the remaining decisive issues; that no one interrupt her while she did so. Paige rolled her eyes; a subdued huffing could be heard in the room. Pat had been very vocal from the start—her hand almost perpetually raised, her abrasive voice often growing louder as she plied us with uneven and insistent contributions. Her tantrum of the previous evening had palpably irritated several people, particularly when it became clear she wanted all of us to sit through nearly a week of readings from the transcript, and this despite being unable to articulate why any of the material really mattered. Everyone consented to give her the floor for an indefinite period, but only after I reminded us that a jury had to reach a unanimous verdict; we would do best to keep everyone on board all the way through.

She spoke for a good, long time, from a list of loose notes, presenting a wide range of arguments and questions. The soliloquy was impassioned. I sensed that Pat was testing out a newly expansive, investigative, methodical, and public version of herself—someone with important things to say about important matters, someone to whom others were obliged to listen—and she seemed to be liking this person quite a lot.

But most others in the room looked as if they were merely suffering her. There was no response when she finished.

For the tenth time we polled, collecting yet another pile of paper scraps, which again added up to inconclusive tallies. Then Adelle raised her hand and began to speak, slowly, seriously, from the corner of the table.

"Last night," she said, "I lay up until very late, thinking about our discussion yesterday. And I found that I kept coming back to this same question: the relationship between law and justice. I realized that what I keep wanting here is for us to figure out some way to do justice, but I am starting to realize that the law itself may be a different thing. What is my real responsibility? The law? Or the just thing? I'm not sure what the answer is. We've been told that we have to uphold the law. But I don't understand what allegiance I should have to the law itself. Doesn't the whole authority of the law rest on its claim to be our system of *justice*? So, if the law isn't just, how can it have any force?"

There was, among some of us, a kind of stunned silence. For it became clear that Adelle had gone to the heart of the matter, directly, and with great equanimity and gentleness. Not everyone could see this. A few hands shot up immedi-

ately, and different people took the floor, declaiming whatever came to mind.

But gradually Adelle's formulation began to take hold.
Several times I asked people to return to it, to think it over,
to repeat back to Adelle what they had understood her to
say. A new question was before us. How could we justify
applying the law if we had decided that the resulting verdict
was itself unjust? I fell out of the conversation for a while,
rolling the dialectic around in my head.

For a moment I feel I have grasped the secret of the system, the perfect illogic of its foundation: the system can fail
to satisfy our desires, and therefore it is a success. In other
words, the true justice of our legal system lies in its ability to
forgo "justice." This, perhaps, is what Aristotle meant when
he wrote his celebrated definition: "Law is reason without
desire."

Am I right about this? Am I just tired? I am not certain.
Still, it seems that it is in the nature of reason to expose fail-
ures, slips, holes—to reveal them. A system that tried to hide
its flaws would be, then, to that degree, less perfect than one
that was avowedly imperfect. If the law could not get the
defendant, then the law made us release him. It explicitly for-
bade us to nudge the rules to get the desired answer.

In my reverie, the failure of the law was taking shape as its
triumph, but when I rejoined the conversation, I heard
growing consensus that the law's only purpose was justice,
and therefore justice had to be the higher principle: it followed, then, that an appeal to justice must trump the minc-
ing details of the law itself. The *law* might prohibit us from
compromising on a manslaughter verdict unless we could
all agree that the burden of proof had been met. But we were
in accord that it was not *just* to let Milcray go unpunished

for what he had done. Conclusion? The dictates of justice demanded that we circumvent the law. QED.

I sensed that people were starting to perceive the law as overly clumsy, somehow—that it was a blunt tool—and that this higher principle, justice, had cast a kind of spell in the room. It had nimbler fingers, could reach into any corner. It was to this more ethereal and nebulous ideal that we seemed to owe our primary allegiance.

Asking to say something, I stood for a moment.

"I just want to make sure," I said, "that we all remember that the weird rigidity of the law, this thing we are all noticing—that it is inflexible, that it seems to let Milcray slip through the net, a net so stiff that we can't figure out how to bend it, to get it to catch this guy—I just want us to remember that there is a *reason* why we have this strange system."

I sensed a kind of focus in the room, a stillness—or was it in my own head?

"There is a principle here," I said. "Isn't there a principle here? That our legal system should be *'blind.'*

"In other words, the stiffness of the law is the product of a very serious idea: that the law should be exactly the same for everyone, regardless of who they are—that our 'rule of law' can never bend, because if it did it could be used to reach and get a particular person, be used to satisfy particular desires. Instead, the idea is that it will be totally rigid, and what it can catch it will catch, and what it cannot must be let go. What I'm saying is that our legal system didn't end up this way by mistake; there have been decisions made to sacrifice the virtues of flexibility in exchange for absolute equality before the law."

I wanted them to see that this wasn't necessarily unjust, it was simply a commitment to a different idea of justice.

Adelle wanted to take us back to the issue of nullification: as we had discussed the day before, we were not, in fact, bound by the law, as I kept asserting.

"What about the Fugitive Slave Act?" she asked, and reminded us that Northern juries in the years before the Civil War had refused to apply laws that required sending runaway slaves back to their masters.

Was I saying that I would have upheld such a law because of the airy abstractions of the "rule of law" and the "equality of persons before the law"?

This seemed to me the first time that Adelle and I had really squared off. Already we were well into the third day of deliberations. The atmosphere was intense, concentrated. Still standing, I said: "This is such an important point. We have to think more about this. I agree with you, that sometimes one has to appeal to higher principles and refuse to obey a law. But let's play out the analogy you've just offered. During the Civil War, juries nullified a law, the Fugitive Slave Act, because they thought it was unjust. We agree that they were right to do so. Let me ask you, then: we're considering nullifying (or let's just say ignoring) a law here; what's the law we would be ignoring by finding Milcray guilty?"

Adelle thought for a moment, and then she said that she wanted to hear what other people had to say about this.

Leah spoke up. "I think I know exactly what law we would be nullifying: the law that says the prosecution has to prove its case beyond a reasonable doubt. That's what some of you are willing to put aside."

This was exactly the point I wanted to make, and I nodded slowly as she spoke, looking at Adelle. When Leah finished, I said that I agreed, that I could see no other way to interpret a conviction, given that I had heard just about all the people in the room (in fact, everyone but Suzy, sitting grimly to my right) say that they believed the prosecution had failed to dispel all reasonable doubts about Milcray's acting in self-defense.

Adelle waved it off, saying she did not think that analogy was correct; she wanted to hear from other people. This was more than an attempt to change the subject: she was earnestly more interested in the group and their opinions than I could make myself be. She seemed to believe in the process—the talking, the exchange of ideas—in a way that I did not.

But now Leah wanted to speak again. As the day had worn on, she had looked increasingly severe and pained. Behind this lay a sense of isolation. Gradually it had become apparent that she alone genuinely believed Milcray's story. Through the afternoon she had been forced to watch as the whole room—even those still supporting an acquittal—had increasingly conceded that he was *probably* lying about many things. She seemed to have taken this hard, as a defection, and had withdrawn into a resigned bleakness, her arms folded tightly across her body. The rationale now cited for letting Milcray go—that the evidence, though broadly persuasive, was not *quite* persuasive enough to clear the exceedingly high bar set by the people's burden of proof—clearly struck Leah as thin and technical. She understood the position perfectly, but appeared to see in it some backsliding from what she had thought was growing support for an acquittal. At this rate, perhaps the campaign for a compromise verdict of manslaughter would actually prevail. Now her frustration spoke, in a plea that we abandon all talk of nullification, of compromises, and apply the law strictly—to preserve the rule of law itself.

"I have lived," she warned, "in countries without any respect for the rule of law. . . ." She was referring to a stint in Central America with her parents, who were in the State Department. "It's horrible. People live every day in fear."

Emotion got the better of her, and the plea became increasingly personal: "I had a friend who was arrested by the police in Turkey, and she was raped, and another . . ."

This was too much for several people. There was a murmur that this had nothing to do with the issue, that no one was advocating police brutality. Leah pushed on, talking over the mixed voices to press her point: beware the slippery slope from a willingness to put the law aside in the name of "justice," to a complete collapse of all respect for the rule of law in the name of holy war or righteousness—this was just a tiny step. "Justice," meant this way, was just a pretty word for "what I want to do to you"; the law was what we had all agreed on.

Jessica had had enough. Her advocating a compromise verdict in the name of justice didn't have anything to do with mandatory virginity testing in the souks of Istanbul.

"This is totally offensive!" she burst out, pushing back from the table. Adelle, too, was on her feet, pacing, agitated, muttering agreement with Jessica.

But it was Jim Lanes, normally quiet, who spoke up sharply, exasperated at Jessica's outburst. "If you're so offended, then leave! She's got a right to say whatever she wants. . . ."

Jessica announced she would do just that, and she stormed into the ladies' room, letting the door slam behind her.

Now it was Pat on her feet, shouting. Through all of this, I was trying to calm things down, to stop a full-scale explosion, but the fuses burned too fast. Pat was haranguing, waving a finger.

"Everyone can say anything they want! Always! And everyone has to listen!"

And this, coming from her, was more than a few people could stomach. Still, I was surprised when Adelle wheeled on her furiously, yelling that she should shut up and that we had all heard more than enough from her on every subject. Shocked, Pat cursed Adelle roughly. Foul language flew back. Pat burst into tears and ran into the ladies' room. Leah held her head on the table. Everyone spoke at once. We had flown apart entirely.

Desperately, with all the urgency I could manage, I hissed for silence. The slamming of the heavy bathroom door echoed in our ears.

"Absolute silence, please . . ." I pleaded. "For ten minutes, please, no one say anything, please. . . ."

People milled around, pacing, breathing. Outside, a wet snow had begun to fall, and at the window one could watch the flakes blow in whirls above the buildings. Looking out, I recalled a break in one of the first days of the trial, when I had stared down at the ground from the window near the elevators. In the even, white field of the snow-filled park, a group of children were playing football. Their two opposing lines converged on the kickoff, and in the clear distance the Williamsburg Bridge reached across the East River. The world beyond the trial. From the fifteenth floor the children were specks, playing, and the distance of this play—free winter play and the thudding of bodies, steam-warm and padded from the frost—made the heart ache. For us, all play had passed away. We were caught in the serious business of adulthood, in wrecked lives, and the wrecking of lives. This was where we found ourselves.

A few times people began to speak, and I asked them to wait, asked them to give us a few more minutes to collect ourselves. The silence was good. It held us and bound us in a manageable common task: saying nothing. Adelle rose, and went into the bathroom to apologize to Pat.

Then I started to talk, just above a whisper, reminding us of the importance of civility, reminding us of the difficulty of the task, and saying that we ought not be surprised that we were struggling—that these struggles reflected our seriousness, and that nothing less than a passionate seriousness was suitable to the task we faced.

A few times people started to return to what had just happened, suggesting that there ought to be a strict rule that we had to let anyone say anything, or that there ought to be a way, politely, to force someone to stop talking, if what they were saying offended someone. But I waved down those topics, saying I thought it would be better simply to close this last episode and move on with our deliberations.

Then I returned to the issue that had caused the break: the rule of law versus the desire for justice. I asked if I could tell them a story, a brief history that I hoped would make peace in the room.

For almost a decade, a close friend of mine had been at work on a study of the punitive systems of democratic Athens. Her book had been published earlier in the winter, the fruit of an undergraduate thesis and then a doctoral dissertation in classics and political theory. Having been classmates both in college and graduate school, we had followed each other's work for a long time. And, watching the rift open in the jury room, I felt as if I were attending a dramatization of one aspect of her argument. Her point had been, in part, that Athenian concepts of justice were inextricable from the idea of the "desert" of each individual—as in what every person *deserved*. Court proceedings aimed to establish this desert, and juries meted out their punishments accordingly. There was even a back and forth between the accuser and the defendant, in which each put forward to the jury different possible punishments and argued for their suitability.

Now, in an effort to re-establish harmony, I offered this story: those among us who were arguing that we could not let ourselves become slaves to the law were not necessarily arguing against the rule of law itself. The ancient Greek judicial system was proof: one could establish a functioning system of punishment, and a "lawful" society, by charging juries to come up with punishments that fit the individual criminal and the specific nature of the case and the people involved. The odd rigidity of our particular legal system—our obligation to find a verdict within the narrow strictures of the law, as described by the judge; our obligation to put aside any consideration of punishment, or of who this defendant was and what he appeared to deserve for what he had done; our obligation to put aside what we wanted to see happen—this was not the only alternative to chaos and barbarism, but simply the system we had inherited. It worked, mostly, and it was ours, but it was not the only way.

By these lights, the struggle we were having reflected one of the very deepest struggles that human beings had faced, for as long as they had formed societies bound by tradition: To what degree was the law a thing apart from people—an abstract system laid over the messy reality of individuals and their specific situations—and to what degree did the law emerge from the texture and character of people and the details of their cases? We should not feel bad that we were fighting over this issue: we were by no means alone. This was the Roman Law against the Common Law, nomology versus casuistry, the Enlightenment confronting its critics. This was serious business.

Some of what I said was true, some fudged. I knew this, and yet my aim was by no means to teach a course in Anglo-Saxon jurisprudence (what did I really know about all this anyway? not much), but to give a patina to our conflicts, to dignify the opposing positions with historical mantles so that we could make peace, see intelligence in the opposing views, and rise to the occasion of such a worthy disagreement.

In this, the story succeeded. Leah slipped into the ladies' room to make amends with Jessica, who emerged a few minutes later, as did Pat. Adelle and Leah remained apart from us, and I could hear them talking through the thick door.

Dean then raised his hand, and rose to speak. The room remained subdued, and behind him, through the narrow windows, the sky was a humid gray. He spoke with emotion, without hesitation, with simple force.

"I've been listening," he began, "to these things people are saying, and I have tried to pray about all this. Now I've decided what I have to do. I believe Monte Milcray did something very, very wrong in that room. But I also believe that nobody has asked me to play God. I've been asked to apply the law. Justice belongs to God; men only have the law. Justice is perfect, but the law can only be careful."

The statement centered the room. Here was an expression of despair that was a vow of faithfulness; a repudiation of sophistication that suddenly seemed overwhelmingly sage. No one spoke for several moments. He did not try to explain, or to say more. He sat down.

We could give the matter to God. What did this mean? How could it feel so extraordinary to consider this? Yes. To God. Perhaps. Yes.

There was silence.

To my right I heard Suzy O'Mear whisper something. Looking over, I saw that her eyes brimmed. "He's convinced me," she whispered again. It was close to a sob. She said it a third time.

No one spoke, except Felipe, who suddenly blurted out that justice was from God, raising his finger and pointing to the sky. His parroting could not break the spell that had been cast. I stood up and walked to the window, fighting back tears. The room stayed quiet for a long while.

Things were by no means over, but something had changed. For the first time a unanimous verdict seemed within reach. My private commitment to a hung jury wavered. An acquittal beckoned. With the most passionate advocate of conviction dramatically converted, only Adelle remained. And there was every reason to expect that she could be moved. After all, she had voted "undecided" (as best I could tell) in yesterday's poll on the issue of self-defense, and she had never been strident, had always sought to learn from others. Now it looked as if she would be standing alone, and this would doubtless weigh on her. Listening to the sustained mumbling behind the bathroom door, I decided that Leah was probably the most powerful advocate for acquittal, so there was reason to think she would make progress with Adelle in their private palaver.

Pat excused herself and went into the men's room. Since

midmorning, she had looked worse and worse. Her medication had proved impossible to secure, because the pharmacy she had asked the court to contact claimed her prescription could not be refilled. Apparently the court had engaged the narcotics unit for help clearing her renewal, but nothing had come through. She had been struggling with a bad cold-sore for several days, but now a number of ulcers could be seen on her face, and though she had applied heavy daubs of base to conceal these, several had opened in the course of the day, and she had been forced to stanch them with tissue. Her makeup bottle lay open on the table, and she had slumped into morose silence after complaining of an oncoming migraine.

From the men's bathroom came the strangled sound of gags. She was throwing up.

Felipe stood and said that he wanted to leave, and that he would vote for anything that would get us out of the room— he didn't care. He also pointed out that Adelle's opinion couldn't be trusted, because she had been very upset by the photographs of the body at the trial, by the blood and gore. She was letting her emotions get the better of her, he claimed.

"I saw her!" he shouted. "She was crying! I'm telling you!"

Dean answered, advising Felipe to button his lip: "I've spoken quite a lot with that lady, Phil, and I promise you that she is one bright woman. What you just said there sounded to me like something disrespectful of that lady, and I'm telling you right here that I'm not going to allow that."

Suzy jumped in, furiously. She had sat next to Felipe during the whole trial, and had complained repeatedly that when he was awake (which was by no means all the time) he talked to himself without pause, and commented aloud on the proceedings as if he were watching a game show. Not to mention that he had struck up a conversation with the victim's sister in the hall—grounds for a mistrial, if anyone had noticed. Would he please keep his opinions of other jurors to himself?

I added that, from my perspective, he could keep his opinions on the whole case to himself as well, given that he had now expressed a willingness to side with whatever position prevailed. The best thing would be for him to keep quiet for the rest of the deliberations.

For the most part he did, actually. He insisted for a while that I send a note to the court asking that he be excused, but when I finally did (writing only that "one juror wishes to be released"), the judge ignored it. The remainder of the day Felipe wandered around the room, sometimes speaking to no one in particular; later he pulled a Bible out of the coat closet and read a few passages aloud. For a while he contented himself with dropping a handful of pocket change and torn bits of paper on the table, the pattern of which he would then appear to read, confiding to his neighbors that he could predict the future and see into the past in this way: Milcray was innocent, and we would find him not guilty.

We drafted another query, asking if we were supposed to consider only those of the defendant's actions that resulted in the death of the victim. An answer of "yes" would have taken out of consideration the wounds to the back and the flight from the scene, simplifying things a good deal. When the sergeant came to pick this message up, we let him know that Pat had become much sicker, and that she desperately needed her medication. He said he would see what could be done. After he left, Adelle and Leah emerged from the ladies' room, and the rest of us tried to explain what had happened in their absence, what Dean had said, how Suzy had changed her mind.

We were trundled back out into the court to learn the judge's answer, but it added nothing: "The jury will consider all the evidence in the case."

When we reassembled, Paige—increasingly excited at the prospect of a verdict, and having abandoned the idea of a compromise on manslaughter—called for a poll, not on all the charges, but simply on what was now recognized as the decisive question: guilty (of something) or not guilty (on the grounds of self-defense). Everyone agreed, and we tore strips of paper from whatever was at hand—notepads, the paper bags from lunch, scraps of court memos. Pushed into the middle of the table, they made a little rubbish heap. I collected them, and read out the results: ten not guilty, two guilty.

Odd. I had been certain that, after Suzy's tearful about-face, we were down to Adelle alone. I asked the room if the people who had voted for a conviction would be willing to identify themselves. Two hands went up: Adelle's and that of Rachel, the older Jamaican woman. She now believed Milcray was guilty? Yes. But she had been persuaded of the opposite for almost three days—what had happened? She waved vaguely at the floor plan of the apartment, mounted on foam core and propped on an easel in the corner of the room. It was too small an area for them to have fought like that, she murmured indistinctly. There wasn't room for Milcray to get out from under Cuffee. Look how the body lay. The futon would have prevented Milcray from getting out on that side.

This made no sense. We had considered all these points

hours before and moved past them. Cuffee could have slumped forward into that corner, he could have crawled several feet before collapsing into the cramped position where the body was discovered. At no time had Milcray asserted that he slipped out from under the victim in that precise position, wedged in the corner.

The only explanation I could think of for her sudden switch was that Rachel felt much of the drama of the last hours had overlooked her. I sensed strongly that she wanted us to remember she was still in the room. At this point patience was not easy.

Paige could hardly contain her exasperation—she rose with an audible groan and paced the short side of the room. Before she could lose her temper, I jumped in and suggested that some of those persuaded we should acquit ought again to run through the grounds of their "reasonable doubts" for the benefit of those still unconvinced, like Rachel. Would Paige like to start?

She eyed Leah for a moment. Leah and Paige, I had learned that morning, had traveled in the same social circles for more than a year, and shared a number of friends, though they were not particularly close. When jury selection began, and they discovered that they were going to get to sit on the same trial, they said nothing to anyone about their relationship. No one ever asked. In retrospect, it seemed they had cemented a quirky, enthusiastic amity with surprising speed, distributing valentine candies together in the second week of testimony, skating out arm in arm at short breaks in the trial. Their emerging differences of opinion in deliberations had cooled this spirit considerably. Who could tell what was going on in their subtle interactions?

Paige took up the challenge, doing a good job of summarizing the case, though she advocated on behalf of Milcray with an urgency that seemed to me to outstrip her actual interest in the whole affair: she had become increasingly desperate to reach a verdict in the last hours. Later, we would find out that she was supposed to host a wedding shower the next evening.

Whatever her inspiration, she hit many of the best points. Again and again we had come back to the way Milcray described the attack in the videotaped statement, in response to the prodding questions of the assistant district attorney: What had his attacker said? Only that it wouldn't hurt. Did the attacker make any threats? No. Did the attacker ever punch or kick him? Never. Did he have a weapon? No. Did he ever threaten the use of a weapon? No. Did the attacker ever say that he would injure or kill him? Never. Did he say anything else? Only that it wouldn't hurt after it got in.

These answers grew more remarkable the more we thought about them. Given that no one had witnessed their altercation, Milcray was clearly at liberty to give any answers he wished. According to the prosecutor, the defendant was a sly and calculating liar, capable of tailoring precise dissimulations to disguise his guilt. And yet here, if anywhere, was the spot for a few well-placed fibs. If he had invented this tale of attempted anal sodomy in an effort to dodge prosecution for a cold-blooded murder, why didn't he have the good sense to embroider his account of the attack in order to make it more obviously life-threatening? Without any difficulty, Milcray could have asserted that "Veronique" assaulted him with much greater violence (Milcray was, after all, badly injured on the leg as well as the hand) or, at the very least, that she threatened his life. These would have been the obvious fabulations of a defendant seeking sympathy, a savvy criminal trying to confect a safe story. Moreover, had Milcray wished, he could very easily have framed Cuffee, by (for instance) leaving the large paring knife that sat on the kitchen counter in the victim's hand.

The logic of the argument was perhaps perverse, but it had considerable persuasive force: Milcray's story was weak, weaker than it needed to be, weaker than a calculated lie would have been. It was, in the end, improbable enough to leave the distinct impression of truth. The African church father Tertullian coined a phrase for this kind of reasoning in his early-third-century text on the incarnation: *certum est quia impossibile* (it is certain because impossible).

There were other issues, too: the telephone records (which seemed to confirm the chat-line encounter), lingering unease about the thoroughness and reliability of the police investigations, the missing motive. But because we had mostly agreed to consider the case as we would one of alleged female date-rape, much of the evidence (for instance, the testimony asserting that Cuffee and Milcray were lovers) lost its significance. So what? Though we all agreed (except, possibly, Leah) that Milcray had lied a great deal, there seemed to be a straightforward and plausible way of accounting for all of his lies: accept that Milcray, more than anything else in the world, wanted to hide some experimentation with homosexual relationships (and this seemed quite likely), and then all the lies—the story of Veronique on the street, the unlikely timing of the events, the consensus of witnesses placing him on the scene—suddenly made sense, as did his initial reluctance to tell the police what had happened.

But none of this could help with the real question: Why did Milcray do what he did with that knife? Why did he stick it in the chest of Randolph Cuffee? Self-defense remained a very plausible explanation. Not, perhaps, the most probable, but it could hardly be ruled out, could hardly be placed beyond a reasonable doubt.

Rachel switched sides again. It could have been self-defense, she now said. We were ready for another poll, and it looked as if we were down to a single holdout.

A solid bang rang out on the door, followed by the perfunctory order to cease our deliberations. We were being called to assemble in the court.

When we had taken our places, the judge turned to us and read a statement: it had come to his attention that a juror was ill; he had decided to have her taken to the hospital; we would suspend deliberations until further notice, and were strictly prohibited from discussing the case any further until the full jury could reassemble. Dismissed.

It was shortly before 5 p.m. on Friday evening.

The hours that followed were the most painful of the whole trial. A new complement of court officers took charge, special-duty overtimers replacing the familiar faces of the last weeks, those kind guards who, in the long days of sequestration, had shuttled us to meals, brought aspirin to the jury room, and stood behind us at the urinals (we were never unattended).

These new paunchy weekend cops had oversized highway-patrol sunglasses and gonzo equipment belts. They exuded a palpable air of armed delight. On the judge's orders they herded us into a cavernous empty courtroom down the hall, where, for almost three hours, we waited without any sense of what to expect. Could the deliberations be suspended indefinitely? Could we be kept in custody all weekend? What if Pat got worse? Would the judge ever let us go?

These anxieties had different effects on the different

characters. Paige grew hysterical. She spun into a full-out screaming fit at one of the new officers, and wept for some time. Felipe had managed to procure a large cigar from someplace, and he planted himself in a vestibule, puffing deeply. Jim, Rachel, Vel, and Dean seemed most solid; they looked ready to wait out anything. All of us, however, felt the overwhelming frustration of having been interrupted at just that moment: so close to a verdict, seemingly minutes from consensus.

Although perhaps not. Walking (under guard) down the hall from the jury room to our new holding area in the empty courtroom, I had whispered with Leah, who had been looking particularly preoccupied since emerging from the ladies' room. I asked if she was holding up. She made an ambiguous gesture.

"Do you have any sense of how things are looking?" I asked.

It was an elliptical question, intentionally. I didn't want to ask her for a report on her conversation with Adelle in the ladies' room, but I wanted it to be clear I was interested, if she felt willing to tell me how things had gone.

She did not look at me, keeping her bright-green eyes focused down the long institutional corridor. "I don't know what I think anymore," she said hollowly.

So here was a shock. The bathroom colloquy had apparently not gone as I expected. It looked as if Adelle might have won over the absolute vanguard of those seeking acquittal. Incredible.

I took a deep breath, and as we entered the waiting room I reminded myself of my position from the start: a hung jury would be fine with me, probably better than an acquittal. Objective for the foreseeable future? Inner exile. I found a comfortable chair in the corner, faced the wall, put earplugs deep into my ears, and took out my copy of Wallace Stevens's *Collected Poems*. For some weeks I had been making my way through "Notes Toward a Supreme Fiction." This would be an excellent time to shut out the world and do several cantos.

For many years this book had served me as a curious tool: I used it to be close to certain people (the small group of those with whom I read the poems regularly—mainly my wife, sometimes a colleague or friend), and to shield myself from many others. Whenever I put in earplugs and opened Stevens, I was both leaving the world around me and, to a degree, waving around a sign that I was leaving. With Stevens I expressed both affection and distance: to carry the book was to be armed to hold banality at bay, to reject the daily dibbling of unpoetic life; but also to be equipped to find kindred souls. *The Collected Poems*, in this sense, served me as a kind of Good Book.

In this way I carried the book through the initial phases of the trial, reading it alone, at a distance from collective moments as a jury, out of a desire to be apart, but also to find fellow believers and, where possible, to make converts. In the hall in the first weeks, Adelle and I talked briefly about a few of the poems when she asked me what I was reading. Why was "Thirteen Ways of Looking at a Blackbird" so often anthologized? we wondered. How representative of Stevens's work was it?

In the back of the bus on the morning of the second day of deliberations, one of the guards—a short, stocky Puerto Rican named Ernie—asked me about the book. What was it?

"Poetry," I said.

Did I read a lot of poetry?

A fair bit.

He used to read a lot of it when he was younger. In fact, one time they had had a Puerto Rican poet on a jury, a great guy.

We talked a little about the island, my wife's home, and I encouraged him to read more poetry, and to try doing it with another person, so he could talk about what he read. He asked if he could see the book. Taking it, he flipped through for a while, and settled on a shorter poem to try, "The Good Man Has No Shape," a particularly difficult piece. A few minutes later, he handed the book back. It was about Jesus, he said, which was not wrong. I suggested a few other things, and he nodded, saying that what always struck him about poetry was that it meant something different to everyone, "like art," he added.

He said it was soothing. I said sometimes, but not always.

On the next morning's bus, Leah and I sat next to each other, and she asked if I wanted to do a poem together. I said yes, and I chose one of my favorites, "Anecdote of Men by the Thousand," a poem that begins:

> *The soul, he said, is composed*
> *Of the external world.*

And it goes on to express the entanglements of geography and spirit:

> *There are men of a valley*
> *Who are that valley.*

We read our way through the poem together, first silently, and then several times quietly aloud, before going line by line. It was pleasing to do this. Later, at the end of the day, she walked over to me and said that she had figured something out. She alluded to the poem's memorable last lines:

> *The dress of a woman of Lhassa,*
> *In its place,*
> *Is an invisible element of that place*
> *Made visible.*

And she announced that this was why her business had failed. I looked puzzled. "I had an importing company for a while—jewelry, textiles, carvings. What he says, that is why it failed. . . ."

She was certainly right. I was moved by the insight. Objects taken from their places no longer had their power. The rings she bought in Peru were part of Peru; in the village they meant one thing, in the Village, something else.

I wondered. Did this explain why we had been willing to ignore the exhibits stacked in the evidence dolly—the blankets, the robe, the wig itself? Were these "invisible elements" of the scene that had been made visible? Could they transport the place from which they came? The things they had seen? They could not.

Now, in suspended animation for hours, I read Stevens, circling around the seventh canto of "Notes Toward a Supreme Fiction," with its remarkable invocation of the fragility and context-dependence of truth:

> *Perhaps*
> *The truth depends on a walk around a lake . . .*

These were powerful words to read as a juror, locked up in a grim room.

We had been assigned the task of figuring out a *ver-dict*—literally, a *true-saying*, a *truth-to-be-spoken*. But we were obliged to come up with that truth in a particular room: a closed room, with two windows and white walls, facing west, on the fifteenth floor, without carpeting, a room with two adjoining bathrooms. Did the truth depend on the bathrooms? On the windows? Maybe. What truth would we have found on a walk around a lake? Such a walk seemed infinitely far away from Manhattan in February.

A walk around the lake—take the jury on a walk around the lake, or on a walk through apartment one at 103 Corlears Street, or on a walk around that neighborhood, to inspect the holes ripped in the concrete to preserve spatters of blood. Take the jurors on a walk to Lhassa. They get to know one another. What do they come back and tell you? Perhaps the truth depends on the room, on the walk, on the snow, on the number of chairs with arms. All these things, I now saw, were part of the truth that we would speak. I was part of this truth. So was my khaki tie, my bag of oranges, my wife, the sound of Canal Street in the morning. Dean was a part of this truth, and so were the Hell's Angels and the dirt in the aisles at Madison Square Garden. Vel was part of this truth, and so was her boss, the Mattress King of Miami. Stevens was a part of this truth, and so were his poems and their places—Hartford, Key West, the thirteen blackbirds. The verdict would come out of the whole of these things, out of us and our world. If there were gods, their justice might be beyond these streets, these people, these memories, but the ways of the gods were certainly not our ways.

I looked around the room behind me. Leah was sitting with Adelle in the back. Jessica and Paige were with them, and they were all talking in hushed voices. I suspected that

I was seeing a new momentum building for a conviction. Jim was sitting alone, napping. Dean was talking to our guards, who had just caught Felipe trying, apparently, to escape out the back stairway.

The strong smell of cigar smoke had seeped around the room.

Paige approached me. She looked distraught to the point of collapse. Evidently she had made an effort to get a message to the judge directly, saying she wished to speak with him. He had declined, and she had begun to insist on contacting her lawyer, in order to discover her rights. I felt confident this was going to get her nowhere, and told her so.

When the judge had embarrassed me in front of the whole court, I had been so angry that I called a lawyer friend and asked him what would happen to me if I gave the judge a piece of my mind. He said I might well be held in contempt and tossed in jail for quite some time; the judge, he reminded me, had almost unlimited power over his courtroom. I now explained this to Paige, who asked me what I thought was going to happen next. Assuring her that I had no special information, I gave my opinion: "Chances are the judge leaves Pat in the hospital overnight, for observation, and he sends us all to the hotel again, with instructions to show up tomorrow at nine. By that point they have a diagnosis on Pat. If she is OK, then we continue; if not, we probably wait some more."

She blanched. "I can't do any more," she said.

"Well, I'm not really sure there is any option." I shrugged.

She asked me directly if there was anything, anything at all, that I could think of that would get her out of the whole mess. I thought for a moment and said, "If you attacked me, right now, or assaulted one of the other jurors, or possibly one of the guards, that would probably do it—provided it was a good, hard, sustained attack."

She looked at me skeptically for a moment, then blankly. I thought it possible she would make a lunge, and I tensed slightly. The idea of going to the floor with her, in a fury of hair and nails, was not altogether unappealing—it had been several long and stiff days.

She walked away.

It was after seven when we received word that the judge wished to see us. As we entered the court, I cast an eye around the room: the victim's family was there as ever, still grouped in the back, wearing long faces; Milcray sat alertly beside his attorney, who surveyed us as we filed past the bench; the prosecutors looked tired and glum; the judge directed his most piercing gaze at each of us as we crossed the room—it was a studied stare, a honed and perfected eye, practiced for the purpose of discomfiture.

When we had taken our seats, he informed us that doctors had treated our missing juror and expected to release her shortly. He would have the court officers take us to dinner and then to a hotel, and we would be expected at nine the following morning.

Several distinct groans sounded behind me, and the judge looked up coldly.

"Juror number eight, you will look at me when I address this court." He fixed Paige for an additional moment with the lance of his eye, and then returned to his memo.

He would also instruct the officers that, if we so desired, the bus was to take us all to our homes, where we would be allowed to pick up a change of clothes. We would be individually escorted into our apartments, and everyone else would have to wait in the bus as the rounds were made through Manhattan, since only a single vehicle was available; the jury was not to be broken up. We were dismissed.

Except for juror number eight, who would please remain.

Out we filed, and as we crossed the bench, I heard Jim speak behind me, loud enough for the whole court to hear: "We're the prisoners now!"

I cringed. Both because the statement rang true, and because I feared how the judge would respond. But either he was not certain who had spoken or he decided to let the remark pass, already having one fractious juror to reprimand.

We were returned to the deliberation room to gather our belongings and await Pat's return from the hospital. Once there, I raised the question of whether we wanted to spend the next five hours driving all over the city so everyone could have fresh socks. No one cared. We agreed that we would refuse to go anywhere but the hotel, and that we would insist on eating there, or being allowed to go directly to our rooms if we wished.

When Paige emerged, she looked shaken. Apparently the judge had threatened her with contempt, and the power-lessness of her situation—indeed, the powerlessness of our shared situation—had been made painfully clear. The court officers collected our telephone messages, and went out to dial them in.

On a torn piece of lined paper I wrote: "Graham will not be home tonight, and it is not clear when he will be. He sends his most sincere love, and requests your prayers."

The scrap came back to me later, marked: "OK left message on recorder 7:33pm J.J."

We piled into the bus, where Pat awaited us, looking

much better. I sat next to Rachel. In the dark, lurching, the tenor of the murmuring conversations suggested that the end was within our grasp.

When we reached the hotel, I went straight to the room and stayed there. Most of the jurors went down to dinner in the lobby restaurant. A guard sat in a chair outside my door; I could see him, in a fish-eyed view, through the spy hole. I showered, ate my last orange, a fennel bulb, and a few almonds, and fell into a deep sleep.

9. The Final Day

I awoke suddenly, before the sun was up, and took my note-book off the night table. I had decided that I was going to make a push, first thing in the day's deliberations, for a unanimous verdict of acquittal.

Why? I am still not sure.

For the first three days, I had tried to maintain some semblance of balance, if not real neutrality. In part, this came out of concern for my role as foreman, as the person responsible for conducting the deliberations. If that person became too vehemently partisan, I thought, there would be a real danger that those holding opposing positions would turn against the process itself. Since my authority (such as it was) rested on nothing other than people's good will, it seemed most important, whenever possible, to let others actually make the case on behalf of the defense.

At the same time, of course, my opposition to conviction had grown increasingly clear both to me and to others: I had hazarded a number of actual arguments for acquittal, and at several moments even tried to tip the format of our deliberations in favor of such an outcome. But through all this, I stopped short of pulling out the rhetorical stops in zealously demanding that we find Milcray not guilty.

Mostly this was because I never felt truly hungry for an acquittal. How could I, when nothing would shake my sense that reasonable people could disagree on this case? I was opposed to a guilty verdict, yes, but if, on the second day, everyone in the room had suddenly hummed in unison and called vigorously for acquittal on all counts, I can't say for certain that I wouldn't have flip-flopped and begun pointing at all the flaws in Milcray's defense. The hung jury had been my first choice from the start.

Was there a logic to this ambivalent stance? Perhaps.

I realize now that for me—a humanist, an academic, a poetaster—the primary aim of sustained thinking and talking had always been, in a way, *more thinking and talking*. Cycles of reading, interpreting, and discussing were always exactly that: cycles. One never "solved" a poem, one read it, and then read it again—each reading emerging from earlier efforts and preparing the mind for future readings. The same went for understanding the past, for teaching history. Whereas scientists and mathematicians might get kudos for *answering* questions, for *resolving* problems, I had always felt that my work involved the exact opposite project: keeping the questions open. They were different sorts of questions, of course. For me, being a humanist meant committing my life to a somewhat absurd task: serving full-time as the custodian of unanswerable questions (how to live? what to do? how to know? why?); caring for them; nudging them to the fore in a crowded world; resurrecting others, now forgotten; keeping track of long-lost answers. Such questions cannot be answered, but they are not stupid.

But this, for all its beauty (and it is, I believe, beautiful, if also, yes, a bit mad), makes exceedingly lousy training for the grim duty of actually answering—closing definitively—an immensely complicated question with swift, withering, and barbed implications: a question like, "Is Monte Milcray guilty of murder?"

Facing that question, I had immediately embarked on doing what I knew best: keeping the question open. This, I think, is what the hung jury meant to me. By handing the question back to the court—by saying, in essence, "Thank you, very interesting, now go ahead and do all of this again with another class"—I would feel that our deliberations had remained an exercise of thought, a splendid instance of thinking for the purpose of thinking. A hung jury would turn our jury duty into a symposium, an intensive discussion group, an interpretive seminar.

Moreover, it would transform the actual trial of the veritable Monte Virginia Milcray—a thing with serious tooth in several people's lives—into nothing but a bunch of words. It would transform the potent proceedings into a long, difficult, dense, and deeply moving *text*—a poem, of sorts.

It could mean something different to everyone. Like art.

I am not certain why, but by the morning of the fourth day this had changed. Perhaps it was because I myself had been worn down and could no longer hold out. But the sense with which I awoke—a sense that it was up to me to pull us together for a verdict—also had something to do with the judge's cursory predeliberation instructions. Though he had informed us that each juror was to hold to his or her own opinion of the case, he had added that we were always to remain open to persuasion, and mentioned specifically that part of the responsibility of the foreman was to work toward unanimity, particularly in a situation where only one or two jurors remained at odds with the rest.

But other reasons suggest themselves. Dean's powerful formulation—that true justice was God's affair—made it possible to imagine, somehow, that the really important question would, in fact, remain open, just as I had hoped. We would leave the complicated question to the gods. This definitely took the pressure off. If the unanswerable question—What is just?—could be deferred, then the trial could be reduced to something much more like a solvable problem—what happens when you apply the law to these facts?

But I cannot omit another possible explanation for my sudden desire to see a verdict. Was it also that I wanted to take over the deliberations? To grandstand? To show I could lead the room to unanimity?

I do not know for certain. I hope not. It is not impossible.

On Saturday morning, the fourth day, I opened my eyes with a sense that, if everything went just right, we could get a unanimous acquittal on the first poll of the day. But I also had a sense that the first poll was critical: if that failed, there was no way to be certain how long things might continue. A considerable weight of anxious anticipation had amassed in the hours since deliberations had been suspended. Brought to bear rightly, that weight could leverage the first actions of the new day. We would not, in the foreseeable future, have a comparable pressure built up behind a verdict. I began to sketch out some notes.

Reviewing that notebook, I can see the different things I was thinking then, as I lay in bed, scribbling by the swing-arm lamp, behind the drawn curtains, the sound of cars already a steady hum outside the window. On one sheet, in a crabbed hand, I wrote:

> We the jury wish it to be known to the open court that we feel most strongly that the strict applica-tion of the law to the facts established by the evi-dence in this case does not lead to a truly just verdict. We have, however, reached a verdict in accordance with our charge.

Farther on I wrote, "There are no trick endings," and then, later still, "We would choose this strong burden of proof . . . b/c the state is so powerful," and beside that, circled, the insight that suddenly seemed to sum up the whole experi-ence of the trial:

> We have seen the power of the state.

This was the thing, I realized. For the last three days, we had struggled to come to terms with the burden of proof that the prosecution had to meet: it seemed unreasonable, exagger-ated, impossible. But here was a way to understand it: the burden of proof was so high *exactly because the state was so powerful.*

All of us probably would have agreed in the abstract, before the trial even started, that the state was powerful. But after four days of sequestration, we had developed a new and immediate appreciation of just what this power meant: the state could take control of your person, it could refuse to let you go home, it could send men with guns to watch you take a piss, it could deny you access to a lawyer, it could embarrass you in public and force you to reply meekly, it could, ultimately, send you to jail—all this, apparently, without even accusing you of a crime.

For (mostly) law-abiding citizens with no experience of the criminal-justice system, with no experience of what it feels like to be made wholly impotent by the force of legal strictures and the threat of legal violence, this discovery had been shocking. One could see the shock in Paige's face as she emerged from her scolding in the court. One could hear it in Jim's angry muttering before the bench. I knew the feeling all too well myself, from sitting in front of the judge as he insulted me and silenced me and sent me from the room when I had done absolutely nothing wrong. At times the encounter felt like the belittling and arbitrary tyranny of primary school: "Who are these people," the child asks, "and how come they can make me do what they say?" Here, in the justice system, your mother couldn't write you a note. It was a giant difference: before the state, there was no higher worldly power.

If we as a jury wanted to understand why the burden of proof fell on the prosecution, and fell with such gravity, we needed only to reflect on what we had discovered directly about the real power of the state and its agents. There was, in a deep way, no recourse. Yes, there were appeals courts, constitutional protections, citizen juries like us. But in the end— in the end there was, simply, the final power of the state. There was always this. This was a power even more terrifying, in a way, than a man with a knife in a closed room. That sort of raw, physical power, for all its horrors, can never extend indefinitely in all directions. If you were to run out-side, people would object, would (in principle) come to your aid. In the room, you know this, even if you cannot actually escape. But there is nowhere to run from the state: it is the sine qua non of such an entity that nearly everyone outside the room (the courtroom, the prison) has already accepted the legitimacy of what the state chooses to do to you (or has at least acquiesced). In fact, all those people out there, they actually constitute the state itself. If you run out to them, they will help catch you. There is nowhere to go.

I began to sketch some remarks, in outline form, that centered on this observation. I was still scribbling when the sergeant knocked on my door to say I had to come down to breakfast. I opened to say that I wasn't eating breakfast; could I please have another few moments? I was working on something important.

No. I was to come downstairs with him. Now.

On the bus, there was a kind of barely concealed exuber-ance. It was a bright and cold winter morning, and the streets were deserted, limed with a dusting of dry snow and pow-dered salt. We caromed over the Manhattan Bridge at top speed, sharing a tacit sense that we would not be doing this again. I scribbled.

On first entering the court building, I asked the clerk if he could find me a set of index cards. It had occurred to me that any way we could distinguish this impending vote from all those that had preceded it would help, and increasing the formality of the process—even in slight ways—might increase the pressure on those who still hesitated. I wanted this poll to be taken on neat and clean cards, instead of the torn scraps that had sufficed to this point.

People had just gotten their coats off and were arranging themselves around the table when the clerk knocked and stuck his head in with the cards. I slipped them into the breast pocket of my blazer.

Returning to the table, standing, I asked once again that we prepare ourselves in a few moments of silence. And when this was over, I began by saying that I knew everyone was eager to take an immediate vote (Paige signaled her enthusiasm and indicated we should get going), but that I wished to say a few words. No one exactly objected.

First, I welcomed Pat back, told her how happy we were to see her looking so much better, and said how hard it had been to lose her right at such a crucial moment. It had been a trying evening without her. I again pointed out how much credit everyone deserved for having done such a remarkable thing: for having talked about such difficult matters with a group of total strangers for more than twenty-three hours. We were strangers no longer.

"Before we go to the poll," I said, "I want to talk about two things, very briefly: first, the burden of proof itself, and, second, how it applies in this case. Let's start with the burden—this is the thing we have struggled with most."

Here I gestured to Adelle. "Many of us feel that this burden is so heavy, so strict, that it may cause us to miss the opportunity to do justice to a person who did a very bad thing. But the question we have to ask is: Why? Why is that burden so heavy? And I think that we all understand why: to protect citizens from the power of the state, from the tremendous power of the state.

"We understand that power much better after the last

four days. We discovered that it is, fundamentally, an absolute power, and a frightening one. We discovered that a man in a chair and a robe could tell us we couldn't go home, that we couldn't talk to our families, that we couldn't even talk to a lawyer. He could send us to jail. We discovered what it was like to be escorted everywhere we went by men with guns. We discovered that, in the end, there seemed to be no limit to the power of the state over us, once we fell into its hands.

"Think with me for a moment. Knowing what we know now, imagine that we had a chance to set up our own state, to make a government, the twelve of us. What kind of protections would we try to offer to the citizens? I think, after what we've learned over the last few days, we would put the heaviest possible burden on the state before we would let it take away a person's liberty, and we would do that because we've learned the secret of government: that the state, any state, is, in the end, like a monster, more powerful than everything else. For this reason the burden is so heavy.

"Yesterday, in a moment I will never forget, Dean and Felipe reminded us of a transcendent idea: that true justice, final justice, absolute justice, belongs to God; human justice can only be cautious, not perfect. For this reason the burden is so heavy. And those of us with doubts must continue to vote not guilty.

"Now for the second thing: how the burden applies in this case. Has it been shown, beyond a reasonable doubt, that Monte Milcray did not act in self-defense when he stabbed Randolph Cuffee?"

I began to look around the room, to let the weight of majority opinion sink in on anyone still wavering.

"I have doubts," I said. "Vel has doubts. Jim has doubts.

Rachel has doubts. Leah has doubts. Dean, I know, has doubts. Pat has doubts. Are these reasonable doubts? Are they the doubts of reasonable people? I hope so. Are they doubts with reasons? I believe so. Let me give mine: there is nothing in all these mounds of evidence, nothing, that *proves* Monte Milcray is lying when he says that he tried to defend himself against a sexual attack." I paused. "And this is a reason."

I cannot say how this peroration sounded. I meant what I was saying, but I had certainly crossed into the terrain of oratory—pausing, rounding my sentences, deploying the tropes. Did this matter? I do not know.

Thanking them for giving me the chance to speak, I mentioned that at breakfast I had heard a few people joking about the movie *Twelve Angry Men.* "But I think we have all figured out that there are no trick endings here, no surprise discovery that will suddenly swing down and change everything. Not guilty does not mean innocent. It means something very specific: it means that twelve people could not agree that the state made its case. I believe we are in that situation."

Here I made a bizarre mistake: not guilty, of course, means (in New York at least) that twelve people *did* agree that the state had *not* made its case. A very different proposition. Curiously, at that final moment I described a hung jury, when that was not at all what I meant. No one, apparently, noticed. Not even I, at the time.

Without pausing, I took the cards out of my pocket and passed them around. Felipe started to speak, but Paige shushed him. There was silence as the cards started to come back, each folded in half. I counted them. Nine. We waited, and two more came in. Eleven. We waited. Still eleven.

At this point there was no confusion about who still held

a card. Adelle sat at the corner of the table to my left, where she had now sat for four days. She had a pencil in her hand, and the card on the table in front of her. She was looking fixedly away, up, behind her, out the window.

No one spoke. Paige adopted a contemplative posture, her fingers prayerfully arranged at her brow. Several others closed their eyes and clasped their hands to wait. Felipe put his head down on his folded arms. One sensed everyone in the room concentrating on the blank card in rapt meditation. Adelle breathed audibly, wrote something rapidly on the card, closed it on itself, and pushed it into the middle of the table.

I placed it, consciously and more or less conspicuously, at the bottom of the pile. I wanted the full dismay of the room to land on her if she had voted for a conviction. Then I began to open the cards and read them: not guilty, not guilty, not guilty, not guilty, not guilty, not guilty, not guilty, not guilty, not guilty, not guilty, not guilty. And the last one: not guilty.

The taut silence of the room broke in a gust of relief. There was absolutely no joy, no celebration, no delight. There was only an imprecise emotional surfeit. People were overwhelmed. I think there were few who were not in tears, though I cannot remember anyone's face, because I was choked up myself.

Rapidly, I went to the wall next to the door and buzzed for the bailiff. I returned to my seat only for a moment, to take out a sheet of the paper we used for corresponding with the court and to write on it the message I had been told to send when our deliberations had ended: "The jury has reached a verdict."

I looked around the room. Several people were embracing, and Paige and Leah were gathered about Adelle, saying encouraging things to her. She looked out over the shoulder of someone giving her a supportive hug, and she said suddenly, tearfully, "If we are doing the right thing, why are we all crying?"

At that instant, the knock came solidly at the door, followed by the requisite bark, "Cease deliberations!" The officer swung the door open, and I stood there with the sheet in my hand.

But as I reached to hand it to him, Adelle cried out: "No! Wait, we're not ready! Not yet."

I stood there dumbly, with my arm outstretched and the officer looking quizzical. I hesitated, and then turned to him, apologized, and asked him to leave.

With this back-step, the room teetered on the brink of an irrecoverable collapse. At the prospect of our having just snatched defeat from the jaws of victory, several jurors looked ready to go wild. I returned to my place and remained standing, asking for people to stay calm if they could and to hear a proposal.

"This morning," I began, "as I was thinking about how today might go, I had an idea for a way we might try to express our frustration, our sense that we've been stuck with an impossible task and given inadequate tools. This might be a way for us to move forward. Do you want to hear it?"

I asked, because it was important that I not seem to be steering things overmuch; the moment could not have been more delicate.

Most desperate, Paige took the lead in saying yes.

I opened my notebook: "What we might do," I said, "is

write a message to the court that makes explicit that we are unhappy, in a way, with our own verdict, that we feel we are doing the right thing before the law but something that is not, in the end, really just. I propose that we write a message that reads something like this," and I read them the statement I had written that morning:

"We the jury wish it to be known to the open court that we feel most strongly that the strict application of the law to the facts established by the evidence in this case does not lead to a truly just verdict. We have, however, reached a verdict in accordance with our charge."

I looked up. Paige nodded. Yes. Several other people nodded. Yes. I asked, "Could we all agree to that?" No one said no. Including Adelle.

So that was what we did. As I wrote out the statement, people consoled one another, and conversation turned to how this, at least, would be a way we could communicate our struggle to the family of the victim—let them know that we had not accepted the demonized portrait the defense painted of him but, rather, that we found ourselves bound by the strictures of the law. We could tell them that we were not unsympathetic toward their plea for justice.

I read the statement aloud one last time to the room before I buzzed for the bailiff. Again no one objected. The bailiff came, and he took the sheet from my hand.

And we waited.

In the half-hour it took for the court to assemble, our mournful solemnity gradually brightened into the camaraderie of a parting of the ways. Laughter broke here and there, as the idea that it was over began to sink in. People started exchanging business cards, and someone had the idea that we ought to circulate an address sheet and then get it copied, so we would all be able to stay in touch. A piece of paper made its way around the room, and someone buzzed for the bailiff, asking if he would make us twelve copies. He took the sheet and said he would, and as he left he said that we ought to prepare ourselves because the court was almost ready, and it looked as if we would each need to be ready to speak. That was all he said, and he shut the door behind him.

This caused a tremor of anxiety. We would all need to speak? About what? Surely this had something to do with our note to the court. What would the judge do? The feeling of solidarity had become too strong, however, for these thoughts to cause much concern. In fact, it felt very much as if part of the new spirit of unity among us proceeded directly from the mischievous sense that we had, together, done something that stretched the rules, that we had found a way to talk back to a judge (in particular) and to the system (in general) so set on restricting our voices over the last weeks. Dean joked that he was looking forward to a chance to speak his mind in the open court. Several others took courage.

Then the call came. Thomas Mackelwee appeared, and asked if I had filled out the verdict sheet (the formal document with the list of charges and a double column of boxes to check—guilty/not guilty), and I said I had. It was in my pocket. We entered the courtroom.

After we had taken our seats, the judge spoke. "Mr. Burnett, I have your note here, and I am going to read it to the court." He did so strangely, without the least trace of inflection, slowly, mechanically, pausing momentarily after each word as if to strip the sentences of meaning:

" 'We the jury wish it to be known to the open court that we feel most strongly that the strict application of the law to the facts established by the evidence in this case does not lead to a truly just verdict. We have, however, reached a verdict in accordance with our charge.'

"Have I read that correctly, Mr. Burnett?"

I said he had.

"According to our legal system," he continued, "a verdict must be in accordance with the law and it must be true. Do you understand that, Mr. Burnett?"

I said I did.

"I want you to answer this question, Mr. Burnett, by saying yes or no, nothing more. Has the jury reached a verdict?"

I said yes.

The judge turned to Thomas Mackelwee, the associate clerk of count, and asked him to begin. He approached me, requested the verdict sheet, and took it to the podium. In response to the judge's prompting questions, the clerk announced, charge by charge, what we had found.

"On the charge of murder in the second degree with intent, how finds the jury?"

"Not guilty."

I looked at Milcray, whose head was resting against his hands, clasped in front of him, his elbows on the table. His head dropped when the answer came.

"On the charge of murder in the second degree under the theory of depraved indifference, how finds the jury?"

"Not guilty."

His head dropped farther, and a distinct wailing went up from the back of the room.

"On the charge of manslaughter, how finds the jury?"

"Not guilty."

And Milcray looked straight up, with tears streaming down his face, and his fists clenched in the air before his throat.

The wailing from the back of the room grew louder.

The defense attorney showed no emotion; the prosecutors sat impassive.

I could hear sobbing in the jury box behind me and to my left. The judge spoke more words, the clerk spoke more words. I was asked a question. Was this the verdict of the jury . . . ?

I said it was, aware that the moment was collapsing for me, that I was not able to maintain any distance from what was happening, that I was no longer seeing what was going on.

The attorneys approached the bench for a conference, and we were told that the jury would be polled. Each of us would be asked to affirm the verdict individually. Did I speak? I do not remember. In my mind I hear Leah, to my left. She answered the question clearly: yes, this was her verdict. Then Jim. Yes. He spoke shortly, without a trace of hesitation. Then Jessica. Yes.

And so it went. I watched Milcray, who had again frozen in a posture of silent expectation, his head against his hands, which were again clasped in front of him, his elbows propped on the table edge. The tears were visible, dripping down his nose onto the table. His head again dropped, slightly, each time an answer came: Yes. Yes.

Once Adelle, behind me, had spoken, the thing felt done. But five answers remained. Yes. Yes. Yes. Yes. Yes.

And it was over. We had let him go.

. . .

The judge addressed us briefly. He thanked us for our work, but not effusively. Rather, it was a backhanded thanks, which began by pointing out that in peacetime jury duty constituted the most extensive commitment demanded of citizens. It was a service to the country, he acknowledged, but it was by no means a service comparable in scope to that which had been demanded of the men of his generation, many of whom had been asked to give up not a few weeks, but years, and in too many cases had given up their very lives. We were to be thanked for what we had done. But we ought not leave with a disproportionate sense of the service we had rendered to the republic. Good day.

He was right. I felt, dimly, a new respect for him, a sympathy for his perpetual irritation with the parade of self-indulgent New Yorkers who passed under his bench.

As I stood to let fellow jurors file out in front of me, my eyes fell on the prosecutors. My instinct was to avert my gaze, out of a sense of decorum, not wishing them to see me looking on at their defeat. But at the same moment I realized that my wandering eyes might be interpreted as an unwillingness to look them in the face, as a sign of some uneasiness with the thing we had just done. This would not do. So I made full eye contact, and held it. No sooner had I done so than my initial hesitation blossomed unexpectedly into icy *Schadenfreude*, a feeling of euphoria, a delight at their failure. It had all failed—the mocking tone, the histrionics with the knife, the obsequies and sarcasm. I turned and followed the others out the door.

Back in the deliberation room, hasty promises bounced

back and forth as people scrambled to collect their things: we would meet up again; a reunion, perhaps; let's stay in touch. The sense of exhilaration had not subsided, but neither had people's urgency to walk free from the whole affair. Walking free had taken on a new meaning for all of us. The sergeant stuck his head in without warning: we were free to go, but we had a last decision to make. We could go out the front (walking down the public hall to the public elevators), or out the back, where we would be escorted by a court officer, and would be assured of avoiding anyone who had been in the court. Also, those who wished could talk with the lawyers, who often stayed around and were sometimes interested in hearing from jurors.

We split on this, four or five of us deciding to walk out the front, and the rest preferring to go the other way. For my part, I had no desire to speak with anyone, but I never wanted to wonder if I had taken the back way because of some uneasiness about facing the family of the victim. They—the brothers, sisters, a pastor, and a set of friends and supporters—had been present for every moment of the weeks of testimony, lining their bench each time we emerged from our deliberations, showing us their lengthening faces. I could well imagine what was going on in their heads each time we requested more evidence, or sought clarification on some quibbling specificity of the legal language in the charge. They must have thought the world had gone crazy: there lay the knife; there was the man who had swung it; what more could we possibly need?

I wanted to prove to myself that I felt right enough about what we had just done that I could pass through them and could countenance whatever they wanted to say or do.

And so, after sixty-six hours of confinement, I put on my

coat, shouldered my duffel bag, and proceeded down the narrow corridor that led along the side of the courtroom, linking the jury room to the main hall of the court building. I was not alone, but the group of us who had chosen the front exit neither walked together nor spoke as we made our way out.

In the end, I had prepared myself for more drama than we found. The prosecutor and his assistant were nowhere to be seen. Milcray and his lawyer had not yet left the courtroom. As I passed the double door I could see them through the small window, making their way up the aisle. The victim's family, I suddenly remembered, had begun leaving the courtroom before the judge had finished his closing remarks. It had been foolish of me to think that I would see them here, in this long green corridor, as I had so many times before, huddled together on the low benches that served as the court's only waiting area. In fact, the hall was almost abandoned, dingy, and poorly lit. It was, after all, late morning on a Saturday.

Two women approached, recognizable as members of Milcray's family. One I took to be his fiancée, who had appeared several times in the courtroom and had shaken her head skeptically at damning testimony; the other was an older woman I took to be her mother. The younger woman was carrying a child. As I walked past them to the elevator, the older woman began to thank me, and to point to the child, calling out weepily, "See, this is his baby! This is his little baby!"

Something in the drama rang false, and it goaded me into the elevator after a quick nod. The idea I had taken into my head as I left the jury room—that I ought to give the twelve index cards to Milcray, because they belonged to him, because for him they would have deep significance, because he would understand that they had given him back his life and that they were therefore a precious relic, a sacramental folio—all of this evaporated in the hollow moment of melodrama in the hallway. The twelve cards remained in my pocket, where I had put them when I threw out everything else on the table, cleaning up before I walked out.

Arriving home, I found my wife waiting anxiously. She had gotten back from her trip late the night before, and had spent the morning calling around fruitlessly to figure out in what court building I might be found, so that she could try to bring me anything I needed. We sat together for a while, and I was reluctant to attempt to begin the story of what had happened. So we were quiet.

Then the phone rang. We let the machine get it, but I heard a familiar voice. It was Leah Tennent. I picked it up, somewhat shaky, and said hello.

Her news overwhelmed, brought great relief, cut me adrift.

She had stayed to talk with Milcray's lawyer, and he had told her that he had fought in pretrial motions to have evidence admitted concerning Cuffee's prior record. What the defense had found was a complaint filed by a young man who alleged that Cuffee had molested him. The case had been dropped because the alleged victim refused to press charges, and the evidence had not been admitted because it was judged "more prejudicial than probative."

In the complaint, the young man alleged Cuffee had enticed him to the apartment by posing as a woman and soliciting sex.

"Oh God," I mumbled into the phone, my eyes closed tight, the space inside my head large, dizzying.

"Oh my God . . ."

EPILOGUE

103 Corlears Street

In the weeks that followed, I tried to return to regular life. I started going back to my office at the humanities center, and even vetted a few of the illustration captions for my book. I rescheduled a trip overseas that I had been forced to cancel when the trial dragged into a third week.

Still, things did not really feel the same. Life had been weirdly sapped of its vitality and importance; my work seemed bizarre and insignificant. Conversation with colleagues at lunch—about books, about the progress of our research, about a columnist several of us disliked—pained me immensely.

In the mornings, perched on the edge of consciousness, I found the trial continuing, not as a nightmare, not even as a dark irruption I sought to avoid. There was no blood, only talk. I drifted in and out of sleep for hours, always yearning at first light to return to the world of the dream, which was the world of the deliberations, as if, somehow, I could continue to discharge a task that seemed impossible to close.

The twelve cards themselves featured prominently in these reveries, the folded stack of them rustling through my head as I slept, though in reality they lay as still as a corpse, right where I had left them on arriving home, in a neat pile on my bookshelf, next to a packet of Advil and a cigar box full of pocket change.

I wrote personal notes to about half the jurors, saying thank you, and telling them how much I had admired their spirit through the deliberations. I sent one to Adelle. I sent one to Dean. Leah and I made plans to have a coffee, but they fell through, and neither of us made another effort. For all its power, I never allowed myself to put too much store in what she had called to tell me the afternoon of the verdict. Was it the trick ending we had all wanted? Had the messenger descended in the final act, wing-footed, wand in hand, dispelling doubt, bearing the Truth? I could not really see it this way: welcome as the news was, it ransomed our verdict only by bankrupting its logic, which I had held so dear. Did any of us, in the end, actually think Milcray was telling the truth? And yet, if this complaint was real . . .

But was it? I had no doubt that the lawyer told this story, but who knew the truth? I thought about making an effort to look up the complaint in police records, but I decided it was better to let the whole matter lie.

I did take a day away from the office and walk uptown from home, retracing in reverse the path Milcray took from Cuffee's apartment to Sheridan Square. I wanted to see the building where it all happened, I wanted to see the divots in the sidewalk where the crime-scene unit had pulled up *in situ* blood samples. Each day during the trial the judge had explicitly forbidden us to make this walk, so each step, even now, felt like a transgression. I hung around for a while out-side 103 Corlears and peered through the glass door into the entrance hallway. The curtains to apartment one were drawn, and there was no name on the bell. Someone pulled up on a bicycle, locked it, and went inside the building. I was tempted to strike up a conversation, but thought better of it. No need to alarm people; probably nothing to learn. I found the holes in the cement, and in the asphalt, and probed them absentmindedly. They were exactly where they had been marked on the prosecutor's diagram of the corner. Encour-aging. Or perhaps not. I peered into the storm sewer where the knife had been found, and walked down the block to the Watutsi Lounge. It turned out I had been there once before, when I was apartment-hunting in the neighborhood. I had gone in to pick up a copy of the *Village Voice* in the vestibule.

I was wasting my time. But my time felt like a waste. Con-versation was toothless, books had no life, days were without focus.

This disturbing sense largely passed. But it took quite a while. For four days my whole being had been focused on a single problem; the solution exacted much, demanding my full intellectual and emotional ranges, extending these. It was a shared problem, a difficult problem, and a problem of considerable immediate consequence. It drew on all of me, and all of others, and we were bound by this. Life hands one few such episodes, and they are, in a way, gifts that go on costing.

I got a packet from Rachel, who sent a picture of herself in her security-guard uniform at the National Police Monu-ment, along with a calendar from the Policeman's Benevolent Association and a money order for the twenty dollars I had lent her on the last day of deliberations.

In the spring, late on a Friday night, my wife and I went to the Met to take in an exhibition of the late-medieval German master sculptor Tilman Riemenschneider. The galleries were mostly empty, quiet, and cold. The sculpture was exquisite, expressive figures in bare wood, softly lit in the open, gray space. We wandered through together, but apart, in silence. Just as the museum was starting to close, and we were leaving the gallery, there was Adelle, dressed elegantly in black, looking lovely, accompanied by a set of fellow medievalists on an outing to see the show. I introduced her to my wife; I asked how she was. She was well, and she thanked me for my note. Had she adjusted to life as usual again? More or less.

The guards asked us to move along. Her group was headed to dinner, as were we. We would keep in touch, yes? Yes. And we said goodbye.

As we made our separate ways out, I thought: "Life as usual again? More or less."

More or less.

And in the mornings, I write, telling the story, trying to tell the story; and it isn't until the end, the very end, as I look at the writing, as I leave the desk, that I see (and I see it sharply, suddenly) that the writing has been, all along (without my knowing), the doing of the thing I wanted so badly from the start, that the writing has done the thing I wanted so badly from the start—it has made the trial into words, a thing to read, to interpret, to circle back through. A text. Like art. Meaning something different to each person. Keeping the large questions open.

But the trial was not that.

Acknowledgments

When Robert Darnton addressed the first class of Fellows at the Center for Scholars and Writers at the New York Public Library, he said that he hoped the center would be a place where, among other things, a scholar could come, be surprised, and take a departure; or allow a serendipitous foray to become what it became. This book happened there, in that way. My thanks to this institution, its benefactors, and the friends I made during the fellowship. I owe special thanks to a number of others: Tony Grafton, Danielle Allen, Ariela Dubler, Jesse Furman, Aaron Hirsh, Jim Schulz, Tina Bennett, George Andreou, David Burnett, Claire Gaudiani, Maria Burnett, and, of course, Christina.

A Note About the Author

D. Graham Burnett is a historian of science and the author of *Masters of All They Surveyed*. After graduating from Princeton University, he was a Marshall Scholar at Trinity College, Cambridge. In 1999, Chicago's Newberry Library awarded him the Nebenzahl Prize in the History of Cartography. A 1999–2000 Fellow at the Center for Scholars and Writers at the New York Public Library, he has taught at Yale and Columbia Universities, and is currently an assistant professor in the history department at Princeton.

A Note on the Type

This book is set in Janson, a typeface long thought to have been made by the Dutchman Anton Janson, who was a practicing typefounder in Leipzig during the years 1668–1687. However, it has been conclusively demonstrated that these types are actually the work of Nicholas Kis (1650–1702), a Hungarian, who most probably learned his trade from the master Dutch typefounder Dirk Voskens. The type is an excellent example of the influential and sturdy Dutch types that prevailed in England up to the time William Caslon (1692–1766) developed his own incomparable designs from them.

Composed by Creative Graphics,
Allentown, Pennsylvania
Printed and bound by R. R. Donnelley & Sons,
Harrisonburg, Virginia
Designed by Anthea Lingeman